bloomin'
bulletin
boards

elaine commins, m. ed.

humanics limited * atlanta, georgia

HUMANICS LIMITED
P.O. Box 7447
Atlanta, Georgia 30309

Second Printing, 1987

Library of Congress Card Catalog Number:
83 -81432

PRINTED IN THE UNITED STATES OF AMERICA

ISBN: 0 - 89334 - 047 - 2

contents

introduction

The traditional role of a bulletin board is to display material, usually pretty pictures and children's drawings. But no matter how colorful or attractive a board may be, students only observe it critically on the first day it is posted. After that, it becomes simply visual "muzak" or background decoration.

The habit of using bulletin boards as mere posting zones can be broken if old thinking patterns are changed. From a passive observation center, the new board can become a hub of activity which requires student input. By applying the basic techniques illustrated in this handbook, any teacher can easily and quickly construct dynamic bulletin boards that stimulate interest and promote creativity.

helpful hints

Preparing an attractive bulletin board can be easy if teachers are aware of some of the basic techniques needed. The following suggestions are practical as well as inexpensive.

backgrounds

Backgrounds often change the mood and appearance of a board. Stapling any one of the following materials over the entire board can create an interesting effect:

colored construction paper
corrugated paper
want ads or comic sections of newspapers
material such as burlap, felt, or cotton
gift wrapping paper

maps
tissue paper
fish net
shelf paper
wallpaper

captions

You can construct effective captions easily by using tempera paint with a brush and a felt marking pen. The following two methods illustrate the technique:

Paint letters with tempera. When dry, outline them with a contrasting or darker colored felt marking pen.

ABCDEF

Draw block letters with a felt marking pen, then fill them in loosely with tempera paint.

borders

You can purchase borders in school supply stores or make them yourself from yarn, colored corrugated paper, lace doilies, tinsel, crepe paper, or construction paper cut into designs.

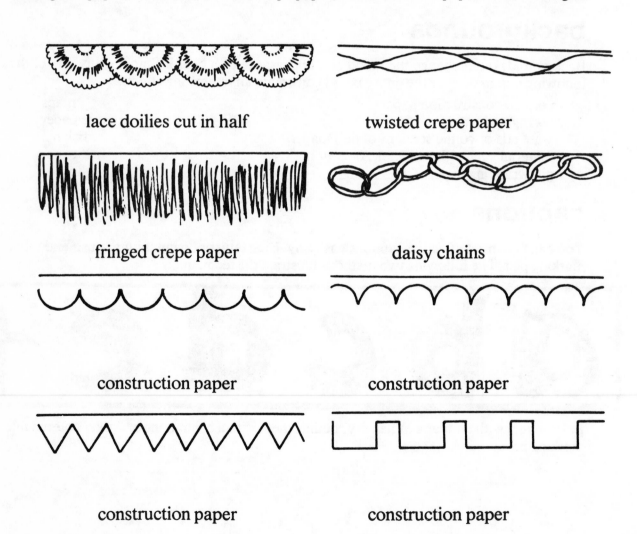

lace doilies cut in half

twisted crepe paper

fringed crepe paper

daisy chains

construction paper

construction paper

construction paper

construction paper

tacking

You can attach pictures and other material to the bulletin board with thumb tacks, staples, or map tacks. Map tacks are less noticeable than thumb tacks, easier to remove, and inexpensive. You will find them at office supply, stationery, or school supply shops.

mounting

Drawings and pictures are more presentable if they are stapled or glued to a slightly larger piece of paper such as colored construction paper, tin foil, or pulled crepe paper. Such mounting creates the illusion of a frame. The frame may be evenly cut, unevenly cut, or torn. The following are suggestions for mounting:

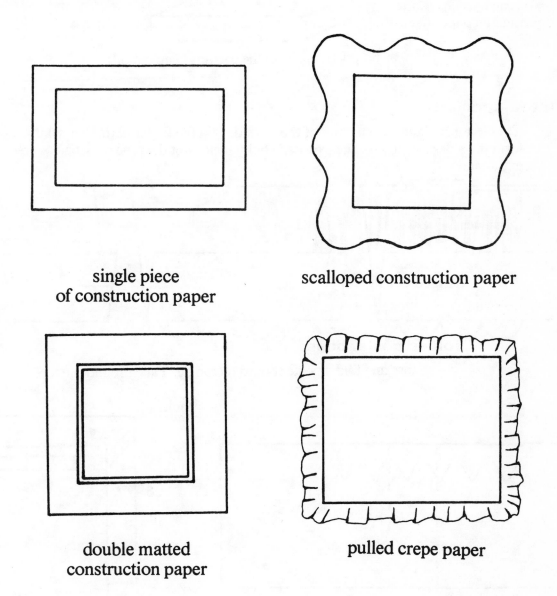

single piece
of construction paper

scalloped construction paper

double matted
construction paper

pulled crepe paper

holders

There are times when you need to provide holders in conjunction with activities on the bulletin board. Holders may be used for holding worksheets, name strips, or other work-related items. They can be any size and, in keeping with the general appearance of the board, they may be painted. The following holders are examples:

cardboard boxes

Use lightweight boxes such as empty tissue boxes (with the top cut off) or the bottom of tennis shoe boxes, by tacking the back side to the board. Boxes that protrude too far should be cut down.

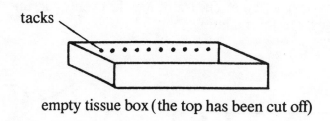

empty tissue box (the top has been cut off)

file folders

Cut off approximately one third of the tab side of a file folder. Attach masking tape to form the sides as shown. The exposed sticky insides of the tape may be covered with extra tape.

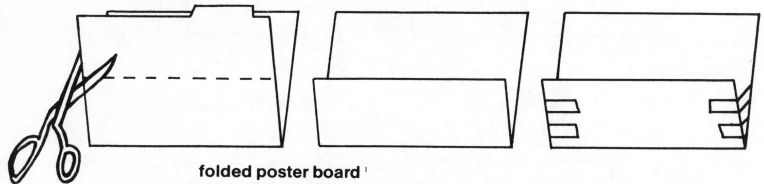

folded poster board [1]

Score and fold a poster board rectangle. Tape around the top.

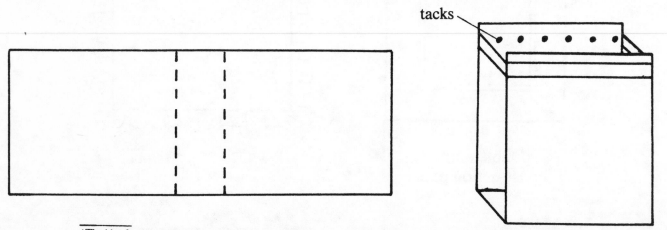

[1] The idea for this holder is from a display kit for librarians. *6 Cartoons, 6 Captions Dozens of Uses* by Mona Garvey, © 1974, by M.G. Associates, 251 Peachtree Way, N.E., Atlanta, Georgia.

clever captions

Many times you can construct attractive bulletin boards around eye-catching slogans or phrases. Post the captions on the bulletin board first and ask the children to contribute material in keeping with the "suggestion" the caption makes. Then post the children's work around the caption. The following are caption suggestions:

My Hero — This phrase may be used as part of a social studies project. Children select their own personal hero and write a short biography of that person.

I Had a Dream — Ask children to interpret, in their own words, what Martin Luther King meant by this phrase.

Right On — Children trace their right hands, feet, elbows, knees, etc.

I'm *Hip* Over — (with an illustration of a hippopotamus) Select a topic, such as sports. Each child writes about his/her favorite sport and how it is played, or about a favorite team or a player on a team. Other topics might include hobbies, vacation spots, video games, TV programs, etc.

Seal of Approval — (with an illustration of a seal) Display homework papers.

Let Your Fingers do the Painting (or Printing) — Post fingerpaintings or printings around the caption.

Hands Off — Post any painting done with parts of the body other than hands, such as feet or elbows. Paintings done with straws or bubbles or string may also be displayed.

And Away We Go — (a transportation board) Ask children to design airplanes (or automobiles or boats, etc.) of the future.

Happiness Is — Post drawings or essays to describe the feeling.

Friendship Is — Post poems or essays about the subject.

Let's *Fall* for — An autumn bulletin board.

***Spring* Things** — A spring bulletin board (Spring is a good subject for Haiku).

Don't Fence Me In — Zoos of the future. Each child selects one animal and draws a picture or writes an essay describing it in its ideal habitat.

Number, Please — This board focuses on telephone talk or the children's numbers. Children might also collect telephone numbers of their classmates, make their own telephone books, and post them.

Information, Please — Select a subject and give the children assignments to describe specific aspects of the subject.

Straight Talk About — drugs, cigarettes or alcohol. Children research the subject and write essays which are posted.

Bon Appetit — Post the children's favorite recipes.

Pick a Card — Write assignments on cards and place the cards in a holder on the bulletin board. Children follow the directions and then you post their papers along with the assignment card.

Fantasy Island — Children write their own "Fantasy Island" story.

Muppets — Each child draws and names a new "muppet" which will be included on a Muppet TV show. Post the children's drawings.

Superstars — Post children's biographies of sports persons, rock stars, comic strip characters, etc.

"Class"-i-fied News — Post information or biographics of classmates.

Acronyms — (words formed from initials such as CORE «Congress of Racial Equality» or NATO «North Atlantic Treaty Organization»). Ask children to create a new organization and make up a name for it which will form an acronym.

Long Vowels/Short Vowels — Divide the bulletin board in half. Label one half Long Vowels and the other Short Vowels. Give each child either one long vowel or one short vowel. Have the children list as many nouns as they can that contain their vowel. Post the lists on the proper half of the bulletin board.

Soft C's/Hard C's — Soft G's/Hard G's — Divide the bulletin board in half. Label one half, "Soft C's and G's" and the other, "Hard C's and G's." Give each child either a soft C or G, or a hard C or G. Have the children list as many words as they can containing their letter sound. (Words may be limited to nouns or adjectives.) Post their lists on the proper half of the bulletin board.

Phonograms — Assign each child one phonogram (anck, all, us, eep, ar, ill, et, um, ell, ent, ou, ake, an, at, ace, ear, eep, eck, ack, etc.) The child writes as many words as he/she can find containing the phonogram. Post the lists on the bulletin board.

Mission Accomplished — Post assignments completed by students.

1

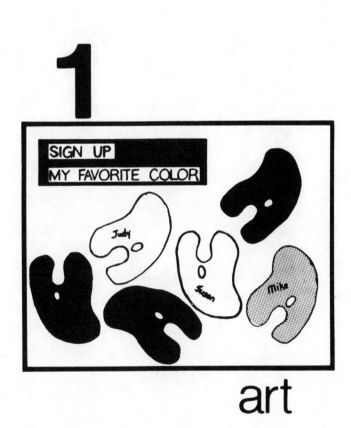

art

Given an idea and the materials for its execution, children *will* create!

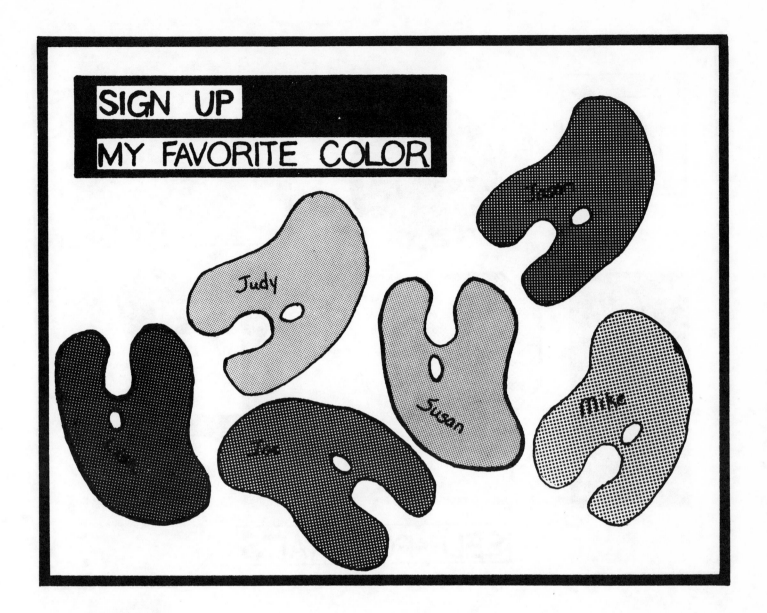

Sign up: my favorite color

Staple a background of white construction paper to the bulletin board. Then cut out an assortment of brightly colored artists' palettes and tack them up. Have the children sign their names on the palette of their favorite color.

Self-portraits

Fill the board with empty "frames" cut from colored construction paper in an assortment of shapes. Make each large enough to hold a child's drawing.

Give the children paper, pencil, and crayons to create their self-portraits. Tack each drawing in an empty frame.

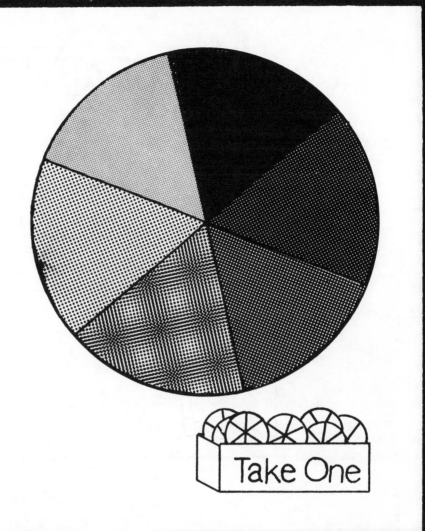

Colorwheels

Staple gray construction paper over the entire bulletin board as a background. Then tack a large color wheel on the board. Attach a narrow cardboard box to the board to be used as a holder for small, unpainted wheels.

Give the children these unpainted wheels and invite them to create their own color wheels.

CREATIVITY

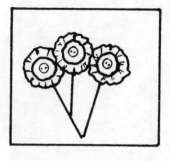

C reativity

Give children two unusual art elements along with manila paper, pencils, crayons, felt markers and/or paint. Ask them to create unique pictures, which you then post on the bulletin board.

Suggested combinations of unusual art elements are:

buttons and paper baking cups (as shown above)
gem clips and cotton balls
paper doilies and egg shells
toothpicks and yarn

Color relay

Put two identical line drawings on the bulletin board. Divide the class into two teams. Give each member a crayon. At the starting bell, the first member of each team goes to the bulletin board and colors in one complete area of his or her team drawing.

When finished coloring, the player runs back and touches the next child on the team. This child repeats the process.

The first team to finish coloring its drawing wins.

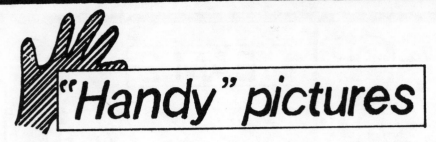

turkey

candelabra

tree

indian

handy" pictures

Give children paper and crayons or felt marking pens. Ask them to trace one or more hands and use the drawing as the basis for a picture.

If children need ideas, suggest such items as those shown:

a turkey
candelabra
tree
flower
Indian

Complete the tree

Staple colored construction paper to the bulletin board as a background. Draw a bare tree with a felt marker and/or tempera. During the fall, have children draw leaves and tack them to the tree and ground.

Further suggestions: For a winter scene, children cut out and tack snowflakes on the board. For a spring effect, children construct leaves, grass, flowers, birds, bees, butterflies, etc., and tack them up.

snowflakes

Cover the bulletin board with dark construction paper. Give children cardboard circles to trace and cut out of typing paper. Have the children fold each typing paper circle in half (1). Then have them fold it into thirds so that it now resembles a triangle with one rounded edge (2).

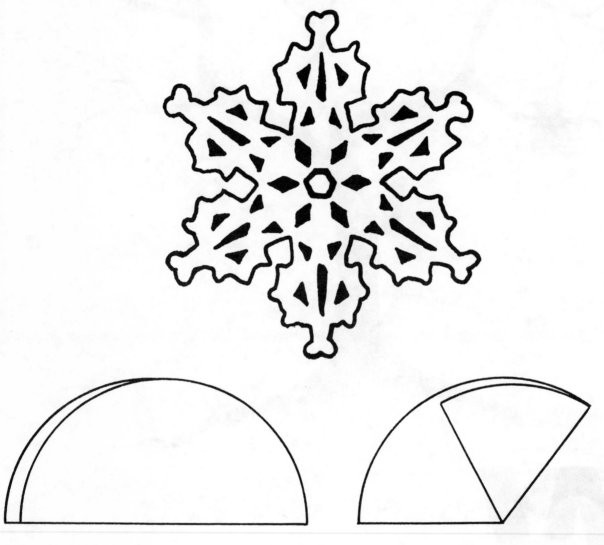

1.
fold

To make six points, cut a "V" from the rounded edge. Then cut smaller shapes out of the rest of the folded paper. (3).

After unfolding the circle, the child tacks it on the "Snowflake" bulletin board. Children usually want to make many snowflakes.

2.

20

Winter silhouettes

Cover the bulletin board with white wrapping or construction paper, and draw a winter scene on it with only a bright blue sky for color.

Cut a variety of winter patterns out of posterboard and give them to the children. Have children trace and cut out their patterns from construction paper, and tack them to the bulletin board.

name the painting & the artist

Obtain several small, inexpensive copies of famous paintings. They can usually be purchased at artists' supply stores, book stores, or museums.

Fold several pieces of construction paper in half. Glue a picture on the outside of each piece. On the inside, print the name of the painting and the artist. Tack the inside half of the lift-panel to the bulletin board.

Schedule this activity to coincide with curriculum studies of famous paintings. After a group lesson, children may test themselves by looking at the pictures, guessing the names and artists, and checking their answers by lifting the top panel.

illuminated letters

Post two or three examples of illuminated letters on the bulletin board. You may also want to display other examples found in books.

Give children pieces of manila paper, 6" or 7" square. They may either trace or draw letters on their papers and then embellish them as they wish. Felt markers and paint will make the letters appear more professional than crayons.

2

R	E	S	A	R	E	L
X	K	S	E	D	I	E
P	Y	U	V	C	T	R
A	W	R	N	S	F	E
I	O	E	N	Z	G	L
N	P	A	P	E	R	U
T	E	A	C	H	E	R

language arts, reading & writing

The youngest through the oldest of students are engaged in the process of learning to communicate through language. This chapter emphasizes intellectual skills such as observing, comparing, classifying, collecting, summarizing, hypothesizing, and creating.

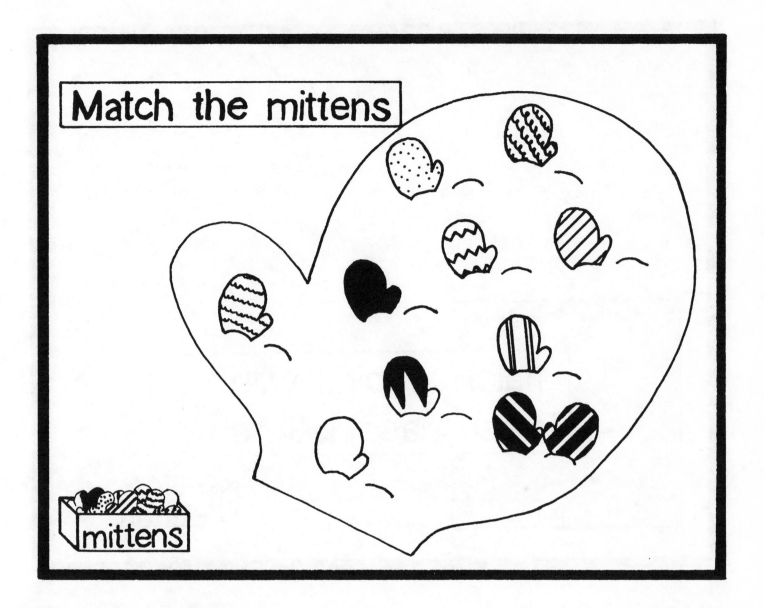

match the mittens

Draw a big mitten on the bulletin board. Then cut out several pairs of smaller identical mittens from samples in an old wallpaper book. Paste one mitten from each pair on the bulletin board mitten. Tack an empty cardboard box to the bulletin board and put the mate to each mitten in it. Children take turns tacking the matching mitten next to its mate on the board.

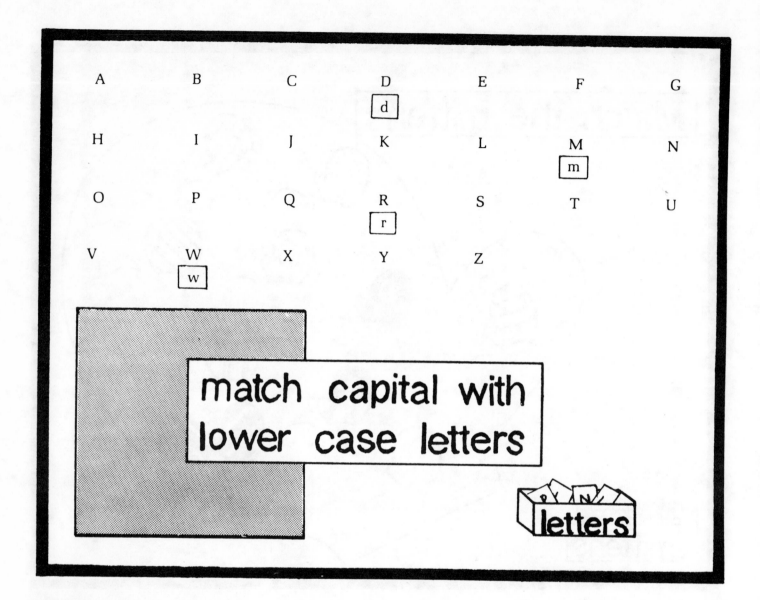

match capital with lower case letters

Print capital letters on the bulletin board. Print lower case letters on cards. Tack an open box to the board and put the cards in it. Have the children take turns tacking matching lower case letters under the upper case ones.

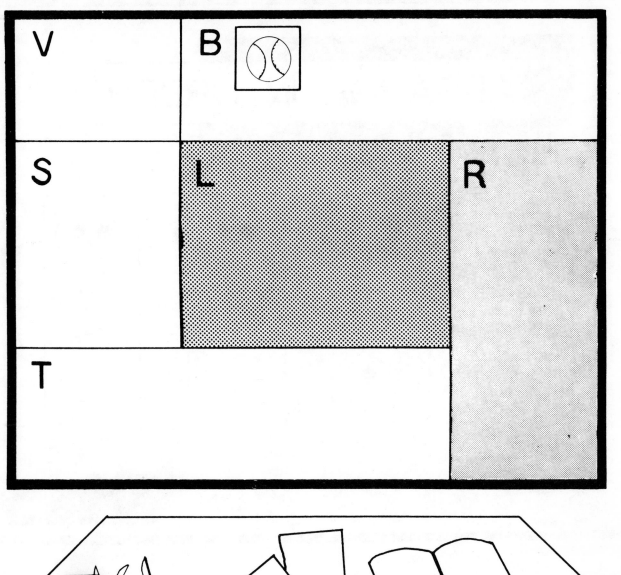

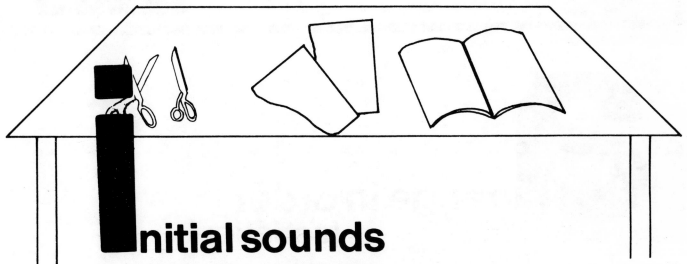

initial sounds

Staple colored construction paper to the bulletin board in sections. Label each section with a letter.

Have children find and cut out pictures from magazines of items which begin with the sound of the letter shown on the bulletin board. Paste or tack the magazine pictures in the correct area of the board.

Further suggestions: This activity can also be used with consonant blends such as ch, sh, wh, etc.

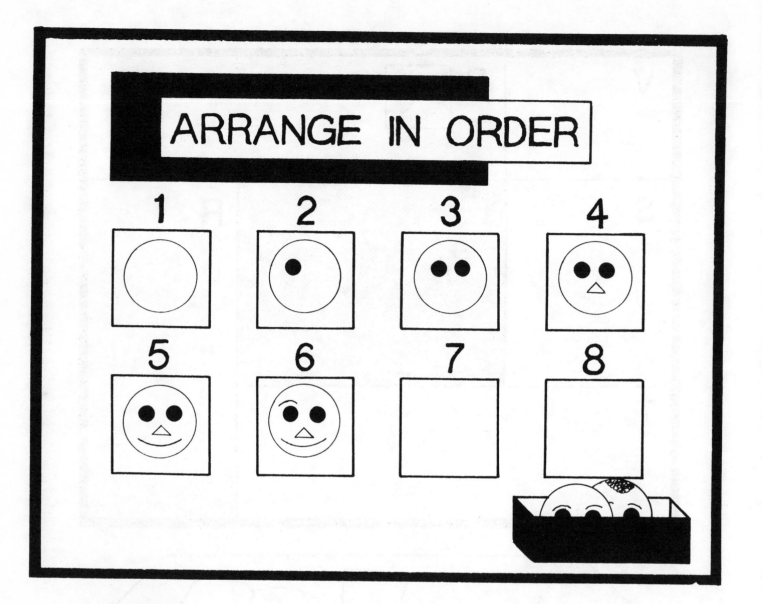

arrange in order
(seriation)

Draw a series of related pictures, each containing one more feature than the one before. If desired, tack a box to the bulletin board in which to keep the drawings. Have children arrange the pictures in order. If you put numbered frames on the board, it will make performance easier for the children.

This kind of board may be designed for young as well as older elementary students.

r ebus story

Draw a rebus story on the bulletin board, as shown. After a class discussion about rebus stories, read with the children what is printed on the bulletin board. Children can then take turns reading it to each other.

Further suggestions: Ask children to write their own rebus stories in conjunction with a specific lesson in either literature or history.

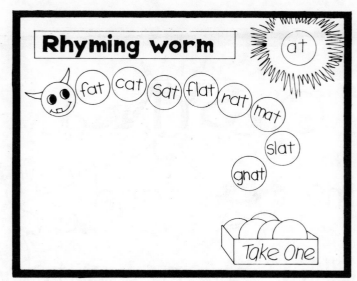

rhyming worm

Print the root phrase used for rhyming in the upper right hand corner of the bulletin board. Prepare a number of blank circles, and tack a box to the board to store them in. Have the children print rhyming words on the circles and tack them to the board to form the worm's body. If desired, change the root phrase daily.

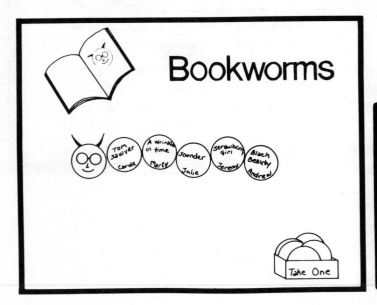

bookworms

In this activity, children print their name and the name of a book they've read on the blank circles to form the worm's body.

SYNONYMS

Synonyms

Children complete the worksheets by filling in the matching synonyms found on the bulletin board.

NAME: _____

big _____

moist _____

icy _____

worry _____

ancient _____

Homonyms

| mist   missed |
through threw	Knew new gnu
rain reign	flower flour	right write
pain pane	two to	one won	by buy
sight site	maid made	peak peek	for four
scent cent			blew blue

WORK sheets

homonyms

Fill the bulletin board with homonyms. The children each take a worksheet. They select any five matching pairs and write five sentences, each sentence containing one pair of the selected homonyms.

NAME: Larry

1) one   won
One student won the prize.
2) _____
3) _____
4) _____
5) _____

34

MIRROR WORDS

give

finish

open

board

seed

work sheets

mirror words

Tape a mirror to the bulletin board. (You can use aluminum foil but it is not as effective.) Print words on tracing paper with a felt-tipped marking pen so the words "bleed through." Copy the "wrong" side of each word and tack it on the board. Children hold the words up to the mirror to read them, and then write them down on accompanying worksheets. This activity is an excellent way to reinforce vocabulary lists.

Once upon a time

Goldilocks

the 3 bears

Hot porridge

their home

the baby chair broke

Storytime

Have children illustrate their favorite portion of a story. Label the pictures and post them in chronological order on the bulletin board.

You may want to outline the drawings of younger children with a felt marker to make them more visible.

Scrambled words

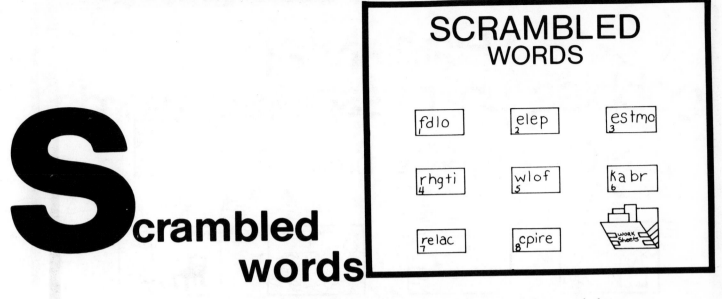

Use words from spelling lists. Number the matching worksheets to correspond with words on the bulletin board.

how many words can you make out of...

Change the word to be used daily if children need additional activity in this area of study. Children post their own lists.

Pac-Man gobbles up misspelled words

Give children worksheets picturing a ghost — preferably lined.

Ask each child to select ten words and deliberately misspell them phonetically on his/her worksheet. For example:

"phunee" and "eelekshun"

Before posting the papers on the bulletin boards, children may cut out the ghosts.

You may want to use this bulletin board as the basis for a phonics lesson.

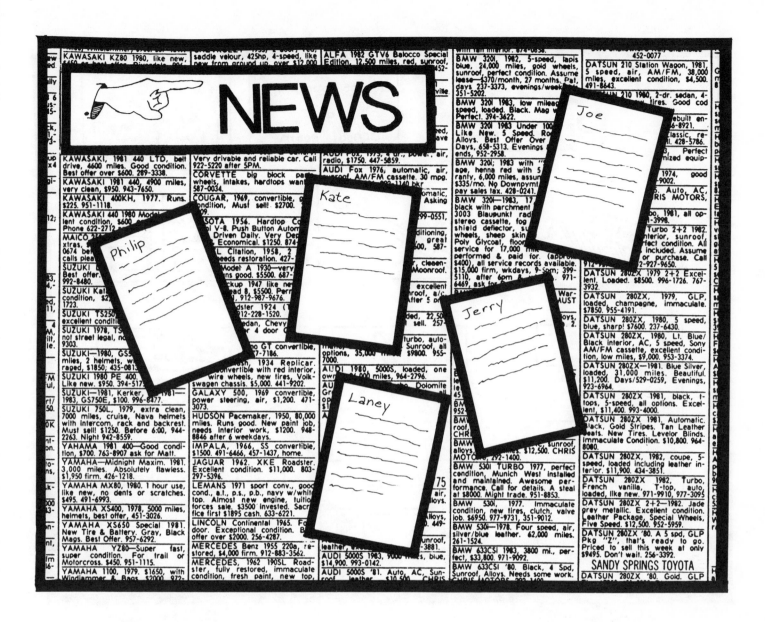

news

Cover the bulletin board with the classified section of the newspaper.

Give each child a sheet of paper with his or her name printed at the top with a felt marker. The children write their own news stories and tack them to the news board. Stories may be changed daily. Young children may draw their stories and then explain them during class discussion.

Ideas for stories include pets, visits to grandparents, family outings, new babies, etc.

Word Puzzle

things found in a school room

TEACHER

ERASER

BOOK

PASTE

RED BLUE GR

Word puzzle

Select a subject. (In the example shown, several pictures of objects that can be found in the classroom are posted.)

Prepare work sheets containing hidden words that match the pictures. (see illustration on the next page) and offer them to the children.

Topics may be changed daily. Other subjects might include things found in a police station; in a beauty parlor; in a doctor's office; at a football game, etc.

R	E	S	A	R	E	L
X	K	S	E	D	I	E
P	Y	U	V	C	T	R
A	W	R	N	S	F	E
I	O	E	N	Z	G	L
N	P	A	P	E	R	U
T	E	A	C	H	E	R

Word puzzle worksheet

Make a grid, then print the names of the objects shown on the bulletin board in the blank spaces. Print names forward, backward or on a diagonal. Fill in the remaining empty spaces with random letters.

The child outlines each word as he or she finds it. The names of objects in this puzzle are: *eraser, pencil, teacher, paper* (appears twice), *ruler, paint, desk* and *paste*.

TYPING

typing

Display stories, copied exercises or nonsense sheets proudly.
Keeping construction paper frames on the bulletin board makes it easy for children to tack up their own work.

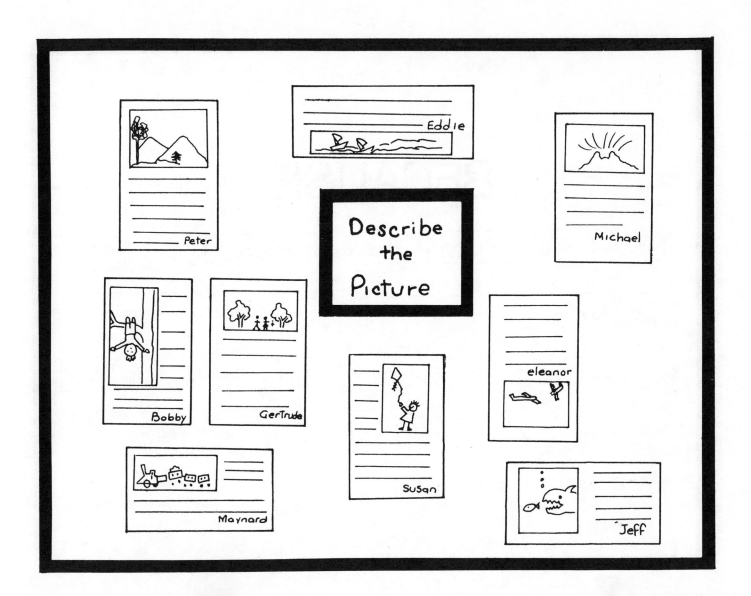

descrıbe the picture

Put a large selection of interesting, colorful pictures cut from magazines on the art table. Children look through them, and each selects one picture and pastes it on a 12" x 18" piece of manila paper.

Children then write stories about their pictures and post them on the bulletin board. Very young children may dictate their stories to the teacher.

BECAUSE

| It is fun to watch TV | because it itches. |

| Saturday is my favorite day | because it smells so good. |

| I hate my new wool Sweater | because they will laugh. |

| I love to bake bread | because I can sleep late. |

because...

Ask each child to write one explanatory sentence that includes the word *because*. Divide the sentence at the word *because* and copy each part on a sentence strip.

Place these strips on a table near the bulletin board. Children take turns rearranging the sentences on the board for all to read.

For example, the following two sentences might be presented:

"It is fun to watch cartoons on TV because they are silly."

"I eat vegetables because they are good for me."

Rearranged they might read:

"It is fun to watch cartoons on TV because they are good for me."

"I eat vegetables because they are silly."

ant, bee, cat

This activity is designed for children in the upper elementary grades. Give the children blank booklets. Their homework assignment is to fill in the pages with words containing the three words: *ant, bee* and *cat*. Encourage them to use the dictionary.

As children finish their booklets, they post them on the bulletin board.

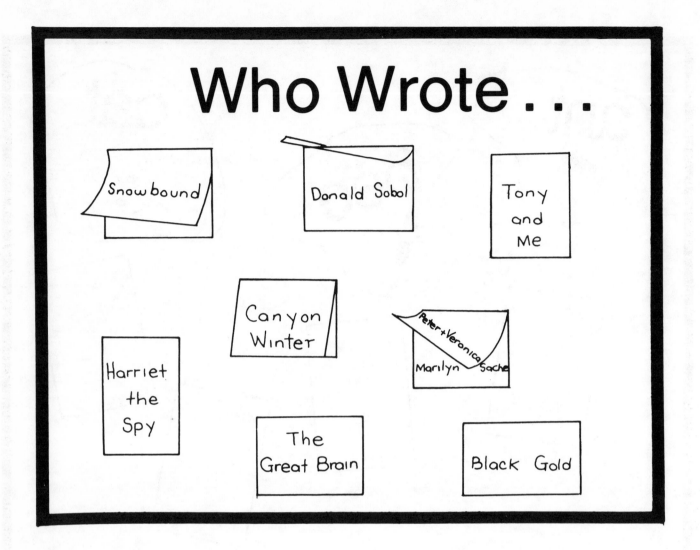

Who Wrote . . .

Snowbound

Donald Sobol

Tony and Me

Canyon Winter

Peter + Veronica   Marilyn Sache

Harriet the Spy

The Great Brain

Black Gold

Who wrote
(lift panels)

The names of books are listed on the outer flap. Lifting the flap will reveal the author.

Further suggestions:

This kind of board may be used for:

1) listing main characters and asking for titles of books;

2) listing authors and asking for the titles of books they have written; and

3) listing musical selections and asking for composers.

letters in space

Tell the children, "Your letter is going to be sent up in a rocket ship to a far away planet. It may be inhabited by humans. What will you say?"

When finished, children post their letters.

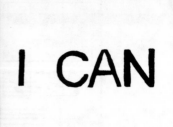

I can write my address, phone and zip-code

_____ _____
_____ _____
_____ _____
338-3838

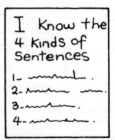

I Know the 4 Kinds of Sentences

1. ~~~~
2. ~~~~
3. ~~~~
4. ~~~~

I can write the months of the year.

January   July
February   august
March   September
April   october
May   November
June   December

I can write all my Classmate names.

i can

Tack up a list of "I can" items for children to write. Each child selects one subject. When finished, post the papers on the bulletin board. (You may also encourage children to suggest their own topics.)

This bulletin board may be used to reinforce any subject in the curriculum. Some suggested topics include "I can":

write all the lower case letters in cursive writing
count to 99 by 3's
write the days of the week
write as many words as possible that rhyme with "at"
name the even-numbered presidents of the U.S. (i.e., the second, fourth, etc.)
name the original thirteen states
write a letter to the newspaper
write a letter to my congressman

Draw a comic strip

Billy

Danny

Amanda

Connie

Joe

Old sayings:

draw a comic strip

Prepare worksheets which contain blank comic strips. Post a list of adages or commonplace sayings on the bulletin board. Each child selects one and fills in the blanks in his or her worksheet to illustrate the saying. Ideas for sayings include:

A rolling stone gathers no moss
A bird in the hand is worth two in the bush
The early bird catches the worm
A penny saved is a penny earned
Silence is golden
Little pitchers have big ears
You can't have your cake and eat it too
A fool and his money are soon parted
Haste makes waste
He who hesitates is lost
A watched pot never boils
Don't count your chickens before they're hatched

dear abby-ann

Ask each child in the room to write (anonymously) two questions to Abby-Ann. Select one of each pair.

One by one, read the questions aloud to stimulate class discussion to reach an answer. As questions are considered, children take turns recording the answers on paper. Post these answers on the bulletin board.

This kind of board is recommended for sixth and seventh grade students.

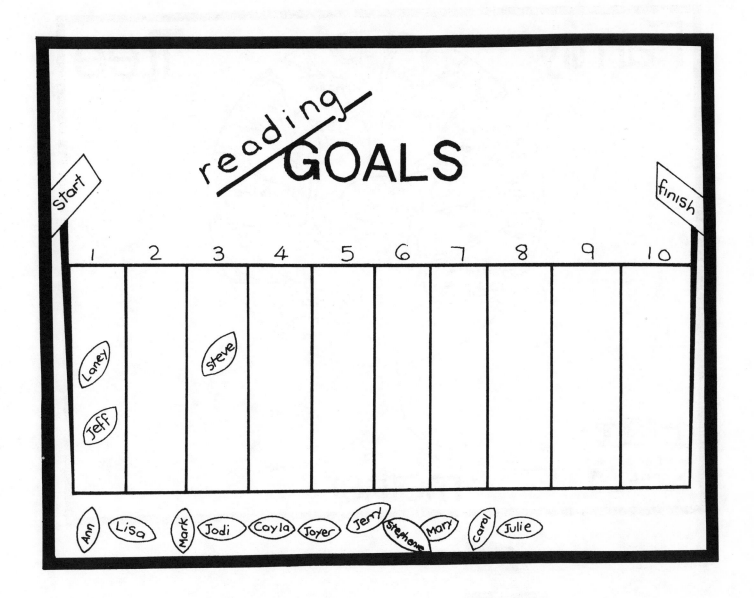

reading goals game

Draw a football field on the bulletin board. Divide it into ten numbered sections. Post one football for each child below the field.

After reading a book, the child places his/her football on the field. As he/she reads more books, he/she advances his/her football toward the finish.

This type of board may include either fiction or nonfiction or both. You may want to provide some type of reward, such as a "reading ribbon" with a small football attached, when a child reaches the finish line.

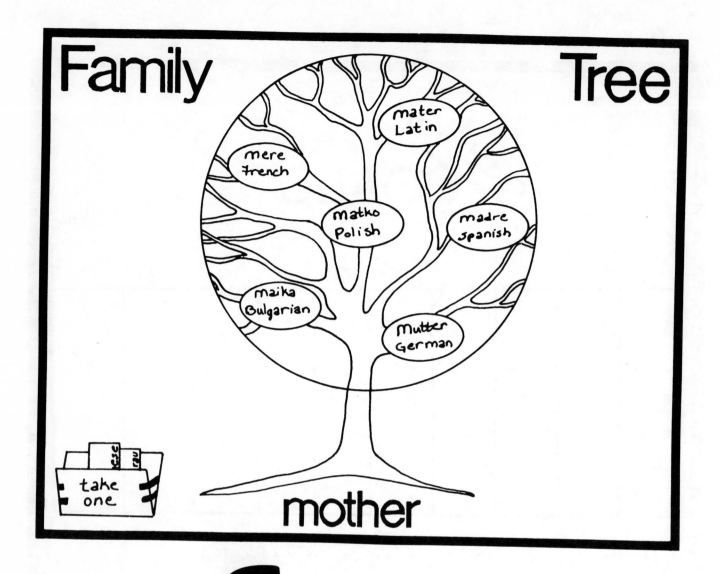

familytree: mother

Post a large tree on the bulletin board. Label the tree with the word for a certain family member (here, *mother*). Print the name of a different foreign language on each of several 5" x 7" cards and put them in a holder on the bulletin board. The child selects a card and writes the word for the family member in the suggested language on the card and then tacks it on the bulletin board tree.

Other family names might include *father, brother, sister, uncle, aunt, cousin* or *grandparents*.

A large variety of foreign languages may be suggested such as: French, Latin, Spanish, Portuguese, Italian, Rumanian, Swedish, Danish, Norwegian, German, Icelandic, Dutch, Flemish, Russian, Czech, Polish, Bulgarian, Sanskrit, Persian, Russian, Greek, Irish, Finnish, Hungarian, Turkish, Arabic, Hebrew, Chinese, Japanese, Malay, plus African languages, American Indian, and Braille.

3

mathematics

Specific math skills which lend themselves easily to bulletin board activities include counting, one-to-one correspondence, matching, recognition of symbols, addition, subtraction, measuring, and estimating.

Count the birds

Sign-Up
Gay 40
mary 24
Philip 42
Joe 39

Count the birds

Children are involved in this bulletin board display from construction of the birds through posting and counting them.

Give the children simple bird patterns to trace, color, cut out, and tack on the board. They may make as many birds as they like. When the board is filled, give each child the opportunity to count the birds and record his /her findings on a Sign-Up sheet.

After two or three days, when all children have made their count, remove the birds. Count them together with the class to discover which student(s) had the correct or nearest correct answer.

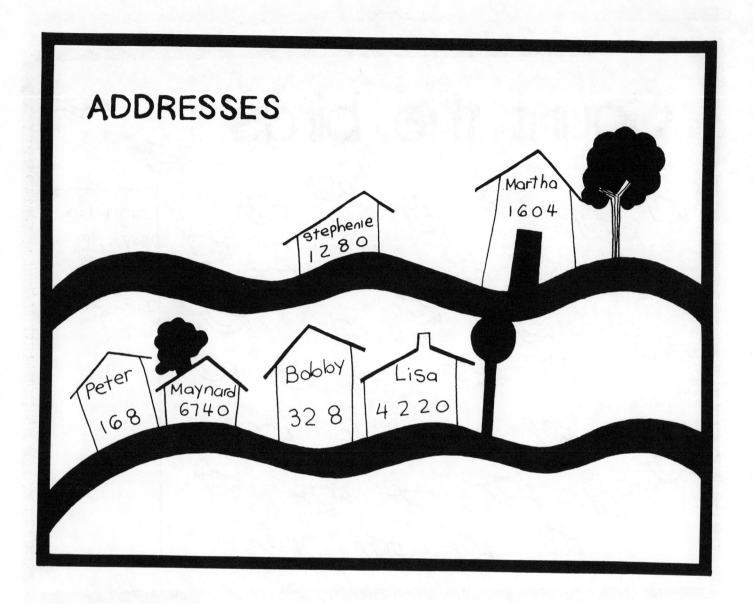

ADDRESSES

addresses *

Prepare a bulletin board background with sky, roads, and grass. Children draw pictures of their houses or apartments and print their house numbers on each. (Help with the printing if necessary.) Then the children cut out their homes and tack them on the board.

* From *Early Childhood Activities: A Treasury of Ideas from Worldwide Sources* by Elaine Commins, M.Ed. Copyright© 1982 by Humanics Limited. Used with permission.

Hang in there

h

ang in there

Tack a box of numerals on the bulletin board, along with clothes-pins and a clothesline, as shown. Children take turns placing the numerals in order.

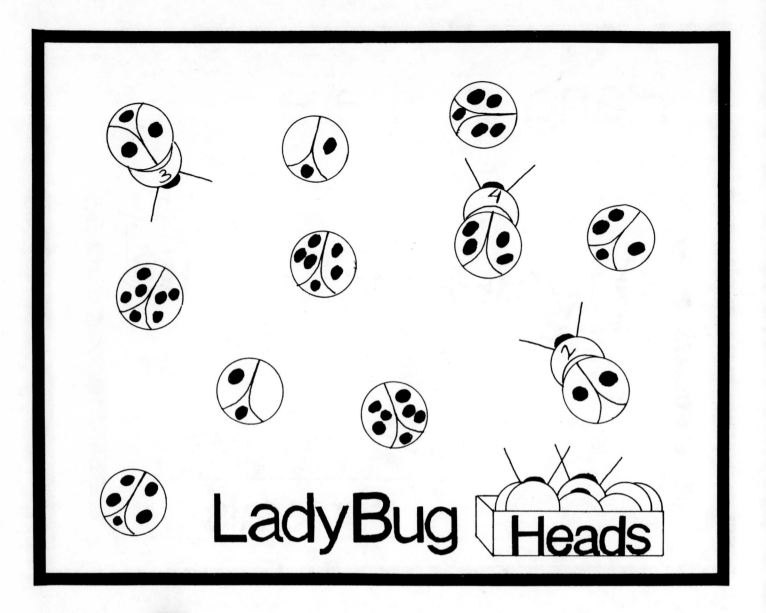

ladybugs
(one-to-one correspondence)

Prepare ten ladybug bodies, each with a quantity of dots on its back ranging from one to ten. Post them on the bulletin board. Put ten ladybug heads, labeled with numbers from one to ten, in a container tacked to the board.

Children match the heads to the bodies by counting the dots.

Add Up Your Number

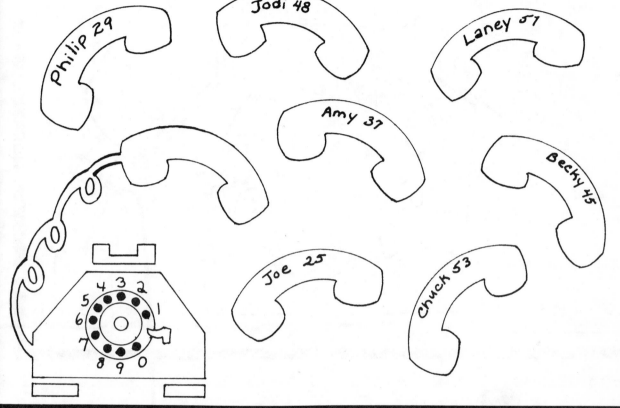

add up your number

Prepare a model telephone as shown and post it on the bulletin board. Have the children remove the receiver, trace it on construction paper, and cut out their own receivers.

The children add up all the numbers which make up their telephone numbers, write the totals on their receivers, and post the receivers on the board. For example, if the child's number is 232-6191, these numbers will total 24.

2
3
2
6
1
9
1
24

dial a number

Cover the bulletin board with construction paper and draw a telephone on it. Tack a cardboard circle, with round openings cut in it for the numbers, over the dial. Attach it so that it may be turned to simulate dialing. Have children practice dialing their own numbers as well as other important numbers. You may want to post a list of numbers.

Science suggestion: Along with the dial phone, attach a tin can telephone on or near the board. To make the tin can telephone, cut off the tops of two cans and punch a hole in the bottom of each. Connect the cans by at least twelve feet of wire, inseting one end of the wire into the hole in one can and the other end into the other can. Secure the wire with buttons. Two children may use this telephone at a time. They stand far enough apart so that the wire is stretched taut between them, and take turns speaking into one can and listening with the other.

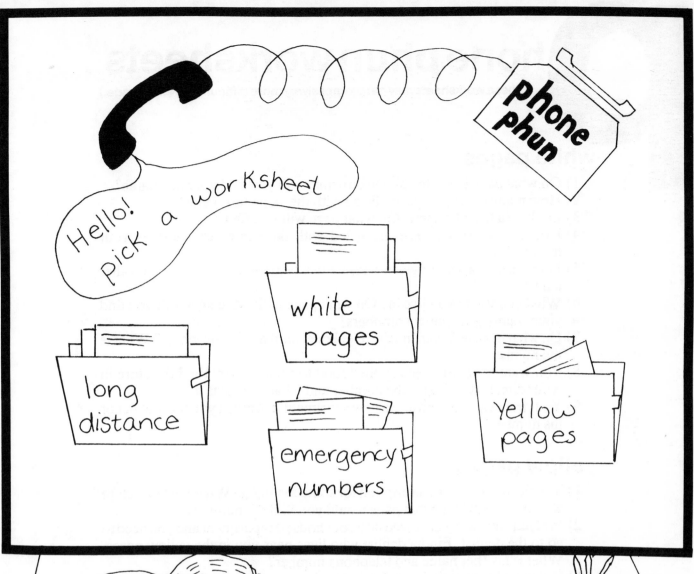

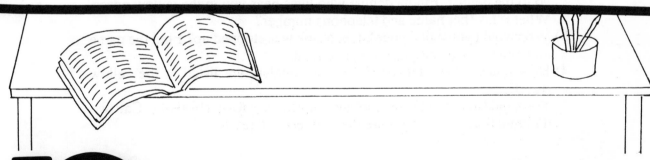

phone phun

Prepare a bulletin board displaying four or five different worksheets to be used independently by students for credit. Below the bulletin board, set up a work table containing a telephone book and pencils. Suggestions for worksheets are given on the next page.

phone phun worksheets

(These worksheets may get progressively more difficult with each grade.)

white pages

1) On what page in the telephone directory will you find your last name?
2) How many other people are listed with the same last name?
3) Look up a friend's name. On what page will you find it?
4) How many other people are listed with the same last name as your friend's?
5) How many pages are given with names beginning with "B"? (or other letter)
6) What county do you live in? On what page in the directory will you find your county government numbers?
7) On what page will you find the telephone number of your school? What is the number?
8) You want to return some spoiled food to your grocer. Find the store in your directory. What is the number and what page lists it?
9) Your friend just moved into a new apartment. How can you find out her or his number?

yellow pages

1) You need to order a prescription for some medicine. What kind of a store would you call? On what page would you find the number?
2) Pretend you have just moved into your house or apartment and you need to go to the dentist. Find a dentist who lives near you in the yellow pages. What is his /her name and telephone number?
3) Who would you call if your kitchen sink was stopped up? Find the name and number of a company to call to fix it.
4) How many Chevrolet (or Ford, etc.) dealers are listed in the yellow pages?
5) You would like to send your mother some flowers for her birthday. Call two different florists and compare the difference in price.

long distance

1) You need to call a relative in Albuquerque, New Mexico but you don't know her number. What number do you dial to get this information?
2) What are the area codes for Utah, South Carolina and Maine?
3) What is your area code?
4) How would you dial direct to New Hampshire?
5) State the hours and days that it is cheapest to make a long distance call.
6) How do you dial if you want to call person-to-person long distance?
7) What states have more than one area code?

emergency numbers

1) What number do you dial to get the police in your area?
2) You need an ambulance. What number would you call?
3) What number do you dial to get the fire department in your area?
4) A cat is stuck up in a high tree in your neighborhood. Who would you call to rescue it?
5) Pretend that when you walk outside your house you think that you smell gas. Who do you call? What is the number and why is this considered an emergency call?

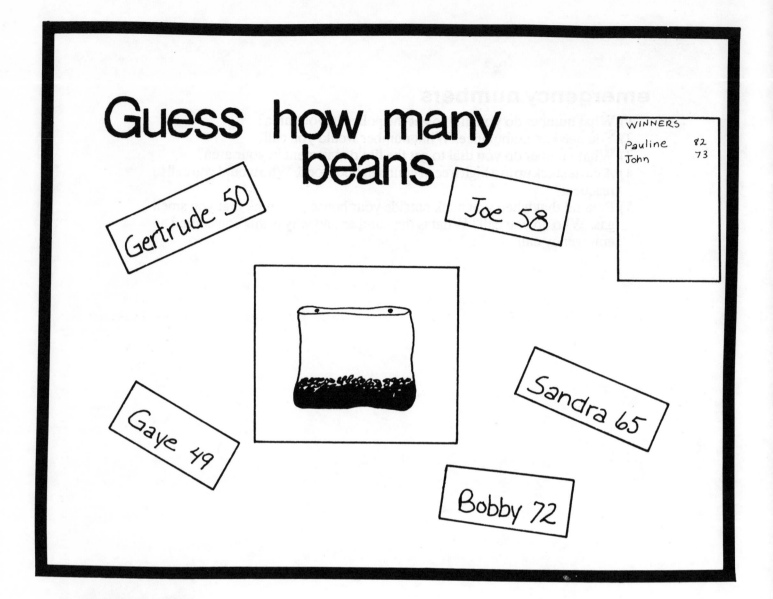

guess how many beans

Put a quantity of beans in a plastic zip-lock bag and staple it to the bulletin board.

Give children blank strips of paper on which they record their names and their guesses. Post these strips on the board.

At the end of the day, count the beans together with the children. The next day, post a different number of beans. If desired, post the winners' names.

guess the number

lift panels

Lift panels are effective when an activity requires specific answers. The following boards illustrate a wide range of topics. If desired, you may post sign-up sheets on any lift panel board for children to sign after successfully guessing the answers.

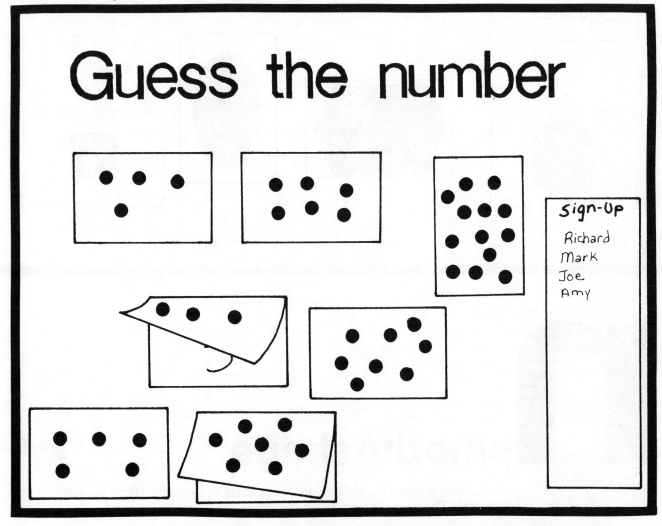

Prepare lift panels with quantities of dots drawn or painted on the outside and the corresponding numeral printed on the inside. Children count the dots on the outers sheets and lift the panels to check their answers. If correct, they may write their names on the sign-up sheet.

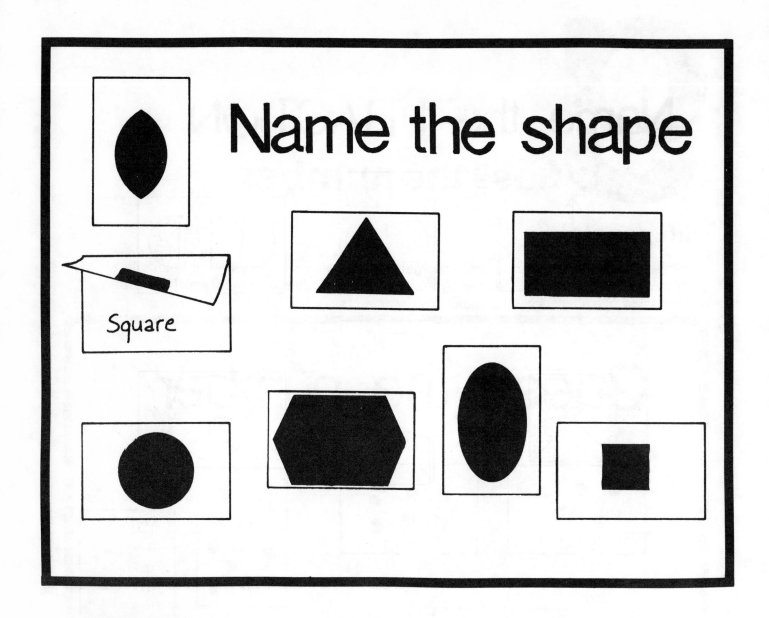

Name the shape

Square

name the shape

Children guess the shape and check their answers by lifting the top panel. The name is written on the inner sheet.

Name the FRACTION

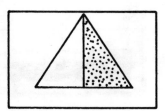
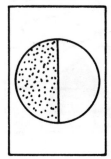
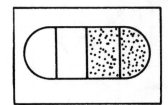

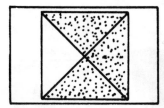
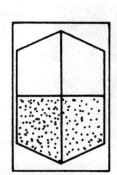
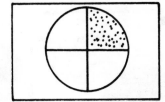

name the fraction

Prepare and post lift panels as shown. Children look for the fractions represented by the shaded areas. The correct answer is written on the inner panel. By lifting the top sheet, they may check their answers.

What time is it?

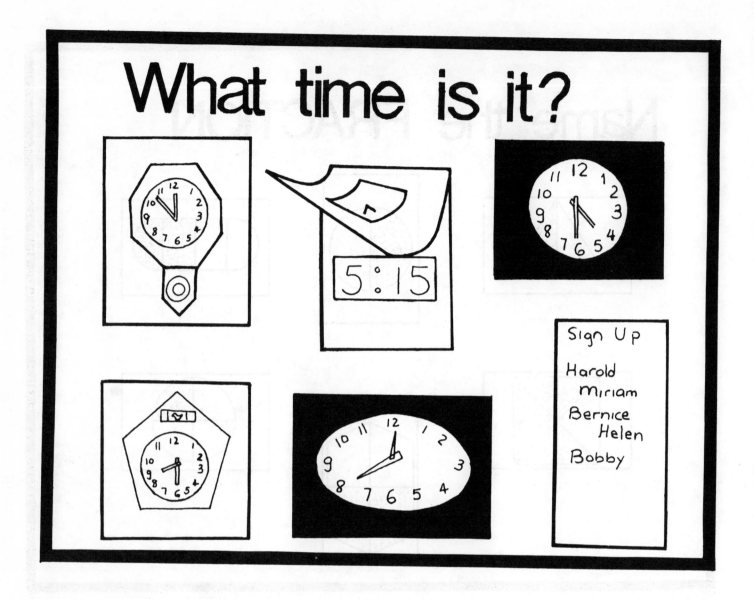

What time is it?

After children have checked their answers, they may sign their names to the Sign-Up sheet.

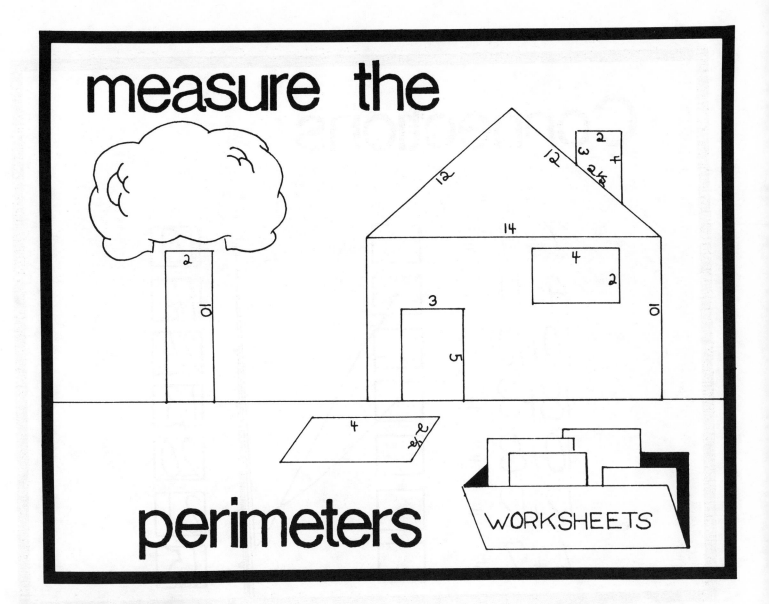

measure the

perimeters

WORKSHEETS

m easure the perimeter

NAME: _____

roof _____

house _____

chimney _____

step _____

tree trunk _____

Prepare the bulletin board as shown. On their own time, children work the problems on worksheets provided in conjunction with this board by calculating the dimensions of various designated parts of the board design. They may turn their papers in for credit. The following is an example of a worksheet:

Connections

$$7+9 = \square$$
$$4+11 = \square$$
$$10+10 = \square$$
$$18+3 = \square$$
$$10+8 = \square$$
$$12+12 = \square$$
$$6+7 = \square$$

| 18 |
| 16 |
| 24 |
| 13 |
| 20 |
| 21 |
| 15 |

Connections

This type of bulletin board is a quiz which can be simple or complicated, depending on the grade level of the children. Addition, subtraction, multiplication, and division may be adapted to this quiz. Children take turns, and if necessary, work problems on paper before connecting the answers to the problems. Check their results. A sign-up sheet is optional.

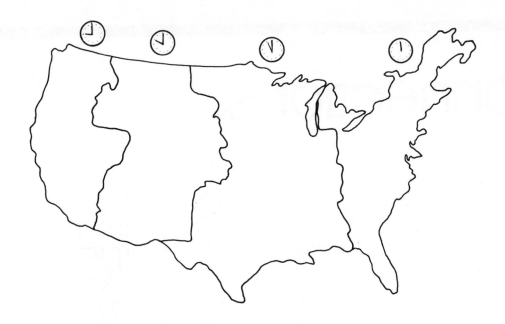

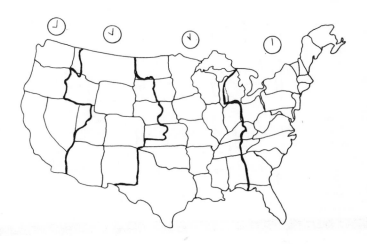

time zones

Combined with worksheets, this board can be used effectively for several days. Change the worksheets daily. The following are ideas for problems to include on worksheets:

1) If it is 3:00 P.M. Central time, what time is it Pacific time?
2) If it is 4:00 A.M. Mountain time, what time is it Eastern time?
3) In what time zones do we find Florida, Texas, Oregon and New Mexico? *
4) In which states do we find two time zones? *

* Provide a map illustrating this information for the children to use. (Enlarge the illustrations above.)

73

4

7:30	8:00	8:30	9:00
Sissy Judy	Ricky Nancy Piper	Brenda Ginger	Guy Joe

health

The key to teaching young children good health habits is promoting an awareness of the subject. Bulletin boards in this chapter are structured to promote awareness and individual participation as well.

7:30	8:00	8:30	9:00
Sissy Judy	Ricky Nancy Piper	Brenda Ginger	Guy Joe

bedtime chart *

Tack a double border of construction paper and fringed crepe paper
around the edge, and use as a sign-up chart for children.

* From *Early Childhood Activities; A Treasury of Ideas from Worldwide Sources* by Elaine Commins, M.Ed. Copyright © 1982 by
Humanics Limited. Used with permission.

get eight hours sleep

Draw a large bed on the bulletin board. The blanket may be a printed piece of cloth tacked in place up under the sheet.

Have the children draw sleeping self-portraits, color them, cut them out and tack them above the sheet.

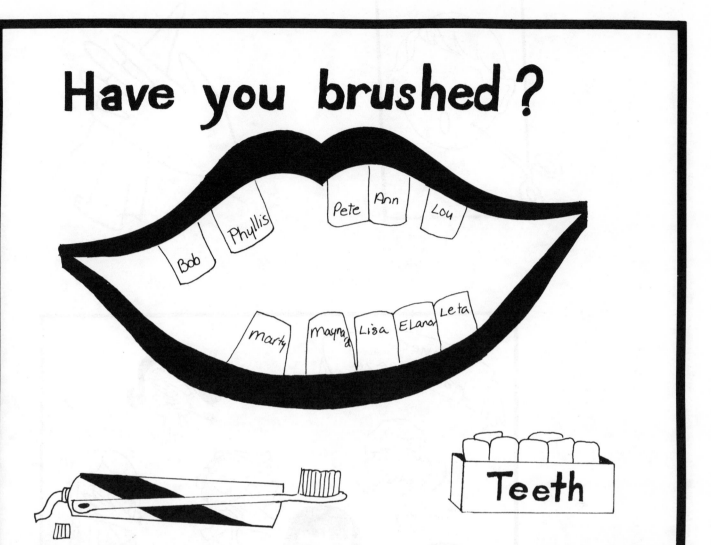

have you brushed? *

Draw or tack a large, open mouth on the bulletin board. After preliminary discussions on oral hygiene, have the children who have brushed their teeth that day take a tooth from the cardboard box holder, write their name on it and post it in the mouth.

Change the teeth daily. This type of bulletin board is effective for about one week.

* From *Early Childhood Activities: A Treasury of Ideas from Worldwide Sources* by Elaine Commins, M. Ed. Copyright © 1982 by Humanics Limited. Used with permission.

Cover that sneeze

Ask children to draw large faces of themselves while sneezing and cut them out.

Then have the children trace and cut out one of their hands and paste it on a tissue.

Tack the heads on the bulletin board and then tack hands holding tissues on each face, covering noses.

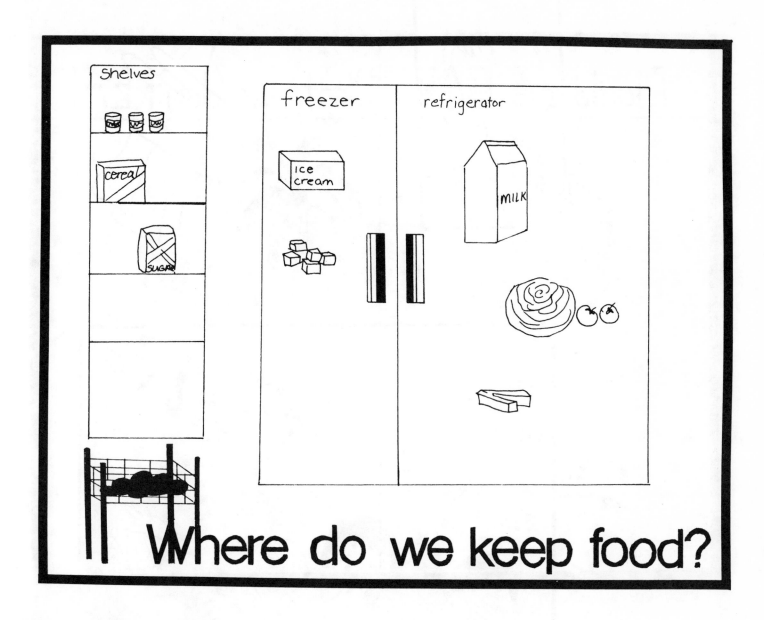

Where do we keep food?

Prepare the bulletin board as shown. Discuss with the children the proper place to store different types of food until they are eaten. Give the children magazines and scissors and have them cut out pictures of food and tack them to the appropriate places on the bulletin board.

| Plants we EAT | Plants we don't EAT |

plants we eat/ we don't eat

Prepare the bulletin board as shown. Have children either draw or look through magazines and cut out pictures of plants. They post their pictures in the appropriate column on the bulletin board.

Further suggestion: Repeat this activity with fruits and vegetables.

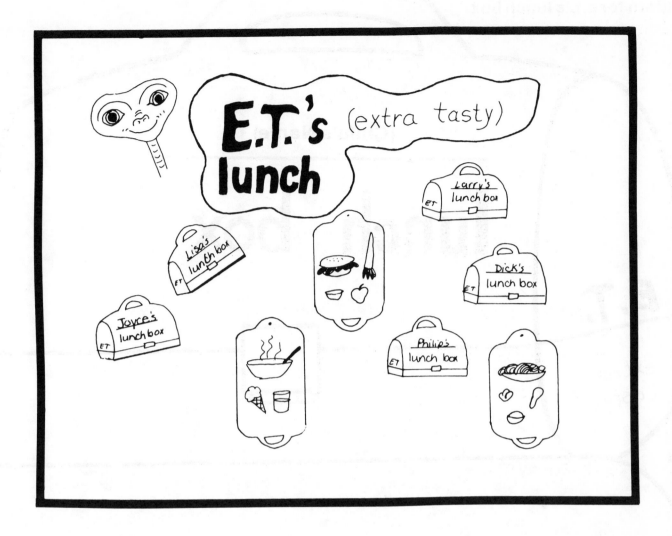

e. t.'s (extra tasty) lunch

Give children a pattern of a lunchbox (see the next page) to trace and cut out. Let them decorate their lunchboxes with felt markers. The children then search through old magazines for pictures of food, which they cut out and paste in their opened lunch boxes.

Have children "close" the lunch boxes and post them on the bulletin board. When children open the boxes, they can inspect the contents and decide if they are nutritious.

Other "E.T." bulletin boards may include:

Extra Terrific — posting of children's papers

Elementary (facts about) — Temperature, or Transportation or Telephones, etc.

Easy Tasks — posting children's math or science papers.

This bulletin board may be used in conjunction with units on food and nutrition.

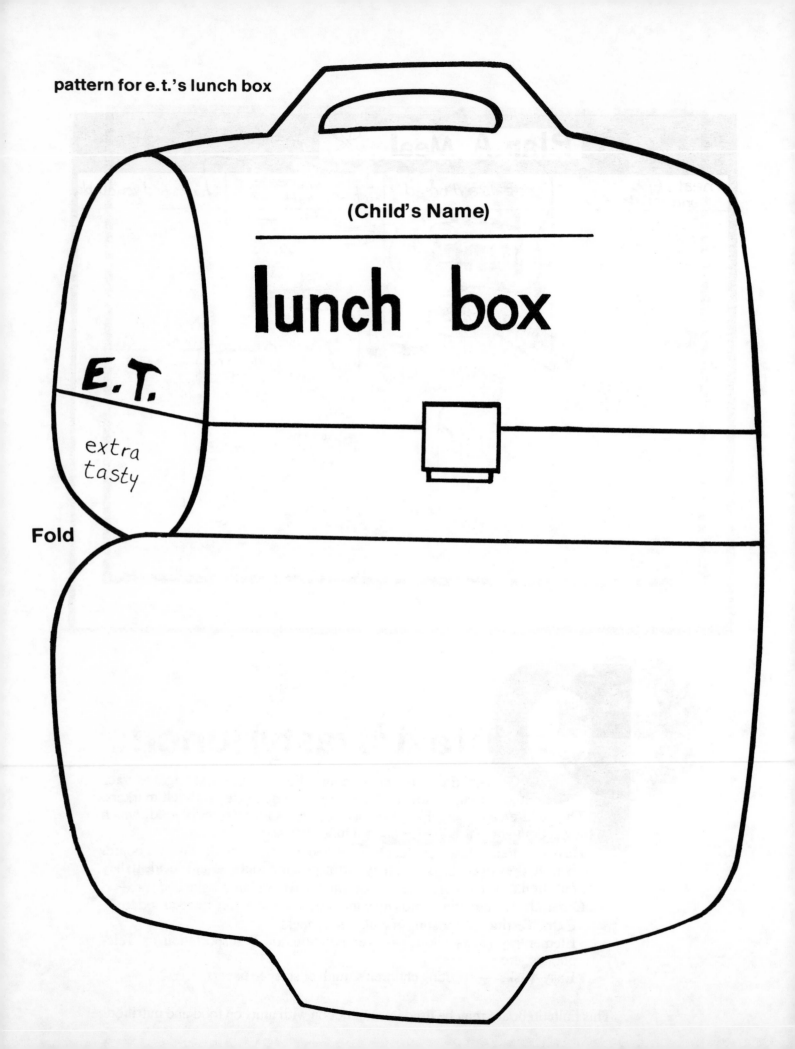

Plan A Meal

meat, fish and poultry	cereals and bread	butter, cheese and milk	fruits and vegetable
.23	.01	.02	.09 soup
.27	.02 CEREAL	MILK .03	.04
.22	.02	.04	apple sauce .05
.15 TUNA	.03	Cottage Cheese .03	Peanut butter .06
.22			.04
.28		.06	.04
.03			.03
stew .16		.04	.02 .04

planameal

Prepare the bulletin board as shown. As an assignment, ask children to use the information on the board to plan a balanced meal while keeping within a prescribed budget. Older students may be required to plan school lunches for a week.

the 3rd grade "chew chew" train

(3rd grade or above)

Staple a background of colored construction paper to the bulletin board. Then tack up a railroad engine on one side. Its smoke contains the caption.

Give railroad "recipe" cards (see pattern on next page) to each child. Have the children print their favorite recipe on their card and tack it up to make a train.

Suggestion: Instead of recipes, children might plan their favorite menu.

pattern for the "Chew Chew" Train Recipe Car.

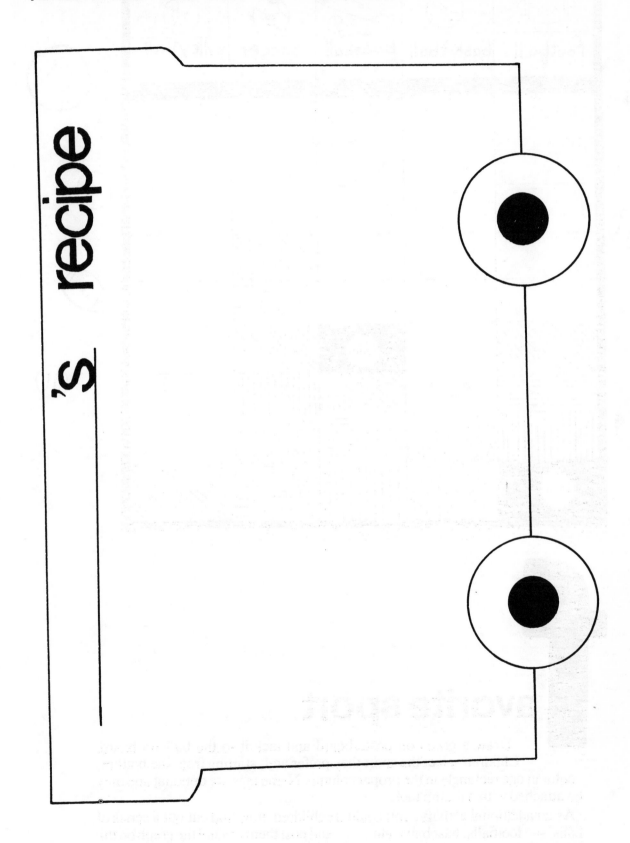

Favorite sport

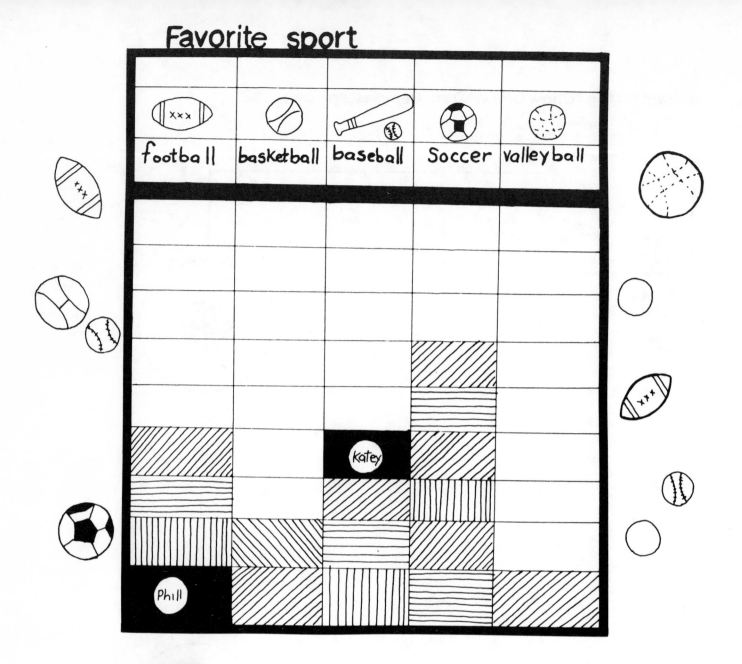

	football	basketball	baseball	Soccer	valleyball

favorite sport

Draw a graph on posterboard and tack it to the bulletin board.
Children select the sport they prefer and, starting from the bottom, color in one rectangle in the proper column. Name tags are optional and may be attached with a thumb tack.

As an additional activity, you could let children draw and cut out a series of balls — footballs, baseballs, etc., — and post them around the graph on the bulletin board.

Further suggestions for graphs:

favorite foods, favorite sports teams, favorite school subjects, etc.

5

Sweetgum   dogwood   white oak   tulip poplar

science

Science is a subject that should invite hands-on investigation and experimentation. The following bulletin boards are designed to promote student involvement.

touch me

All parts of the "Touch Me" board are cut out of various textures such as corrugated cardboard, yarn, felt, shag rug, velvet, sandpaper, cotton, cellophane, aluminum foil and burlap.

For added interest, provide a felt mask so children may cover their eyes as they feel the various textures.

Color Changes

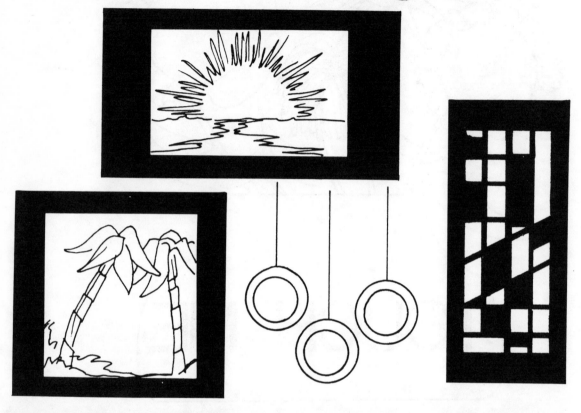

Color changes

Cut out the centers of three paper plates. Staple yellow, red and blue cellophane across the empty centers.

Post three large pictures on the bulletin board, each one emphasizing one primary color. Invite children to experiment looking at the pictures through the cellophane colors. Ask them to describe what happens to the yellow picture when looking at it through red cellophane, etc.

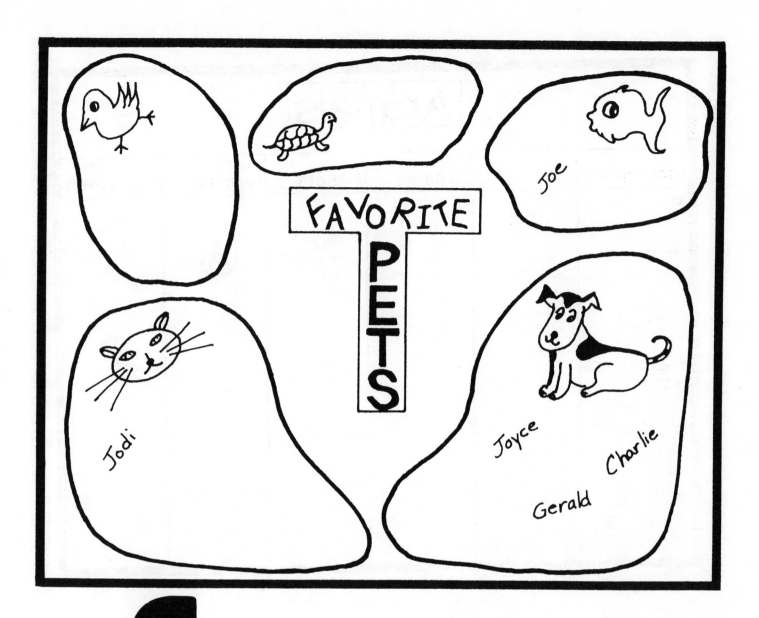

favorite pets

Prepare the bulletin board as shown to indicate a variety of household pets. Children select their favorite pet and sign their names in the designated area.

Animals					
mammals	fish	birds	insects	reptiles	amphibians

animals

Divide the class into six groups. Give each group an animal category to investigate. Draw six corresponding columns on the bulletin board. Ask each group to write a brief description of the animals in their category to be posted in the appropriate column. For example:

"Insects' bodies are divided into three parts: the head, the thorax, and the abdomen. They have six legs."

Ask children to look through old magazines for pictures of their animals, and post these in the proper column as well.

birds

Draw or tack a large picture of a bird on the bulletin board.
Give children feather patterns to trace, color and cut out. (The feathers may be colored randomly or modeled after a specific species.) Tack the feathers on the bird drawing.

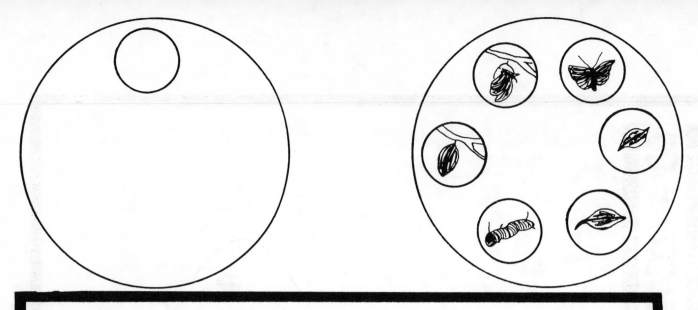

Butterflies

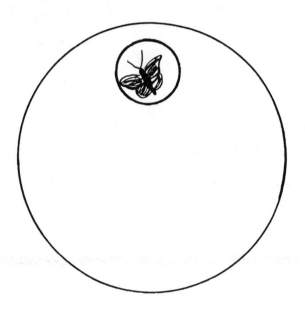

Turn the wheel

metamorphosis
(butterflies)

Cut a large circle out of posterboard. Cut out a smaller circle near the edge of the large circle (1). Cover the bulletin board with colored construction paper. Trace a large circle from the posterboard circle onto the bulletin board. Trace six smaller circles also inside the edge of the large circle. In each of the smaller circles, draw a segment of the life cycle of a butterfly (2). Tack the large circle over the bulletin board circle. Children take turns turning the wheel (3). (The life cycle of the frog can also serve as the subject of this board.)

Create an Animal

Lionagator

Eletiger

Frogilla

Mulefish

Mickeydog

Create an animal

Ask the children to create new breeds of animals. Have them draw pictures of their animals and then describe their unique physical characteristics. They may also describe their animals' habitat, what they eat, how they move, how they sound, etc. Post the children's papers on the bulletin board.

Studying animals

When studying specific animals, encourage children to find out all they can about one particular kind of a species. Suggest that the children find out such things as:

Where the animals live?
Do they have territories?
Do they live alone or in flocks or herds?
In what climate do they live?
What do they eat?
How do they protect themselves?
Do they serve man? How?
How do they fit into the balance of life?
How do they move? Are they fast or slow?
How big do they grow?

Post the children's papers and drawings on the bulletin board. Three different bulletin boards using animals as subjects for investigation are shown here. As an example, the kinds of bears children can study include: Alaskan Brown Bear, Polar Bear, Grizzly Bear, American Black Bear, Asiatic Black Bear, Sloth Bear, Spectacled Bear and Sun Bear.

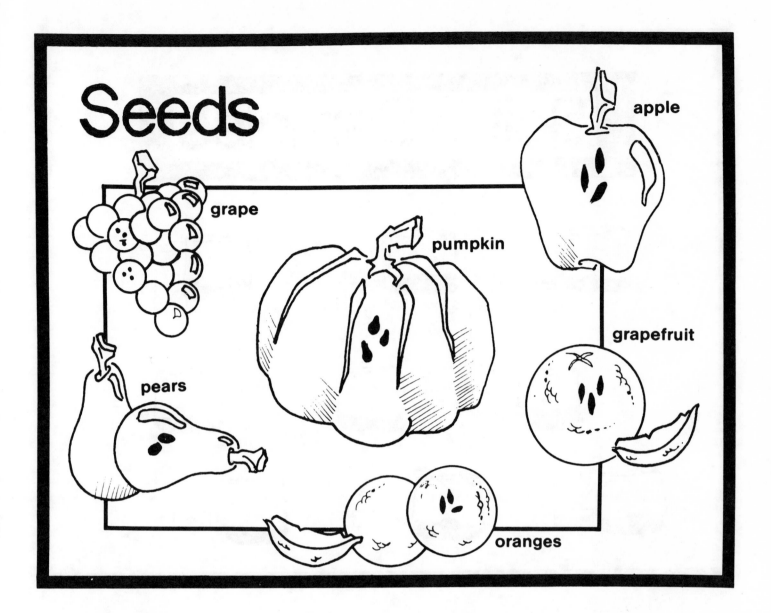

Seeds

grape

apple

pumpkin

grapefruit

pears

oranges

Seeds *

Post several large drawings of fruits that contain seeds on the bulletin board. Ask children to bring seeds from home and glue them to the appropriate drawings.

* From *Early Childhood Activities: A Treasury of Ideas from Worldwide Sources* by Elaine Commins, M. Ed. Copyright © 1982 by Humanics Limited. Used with permission.

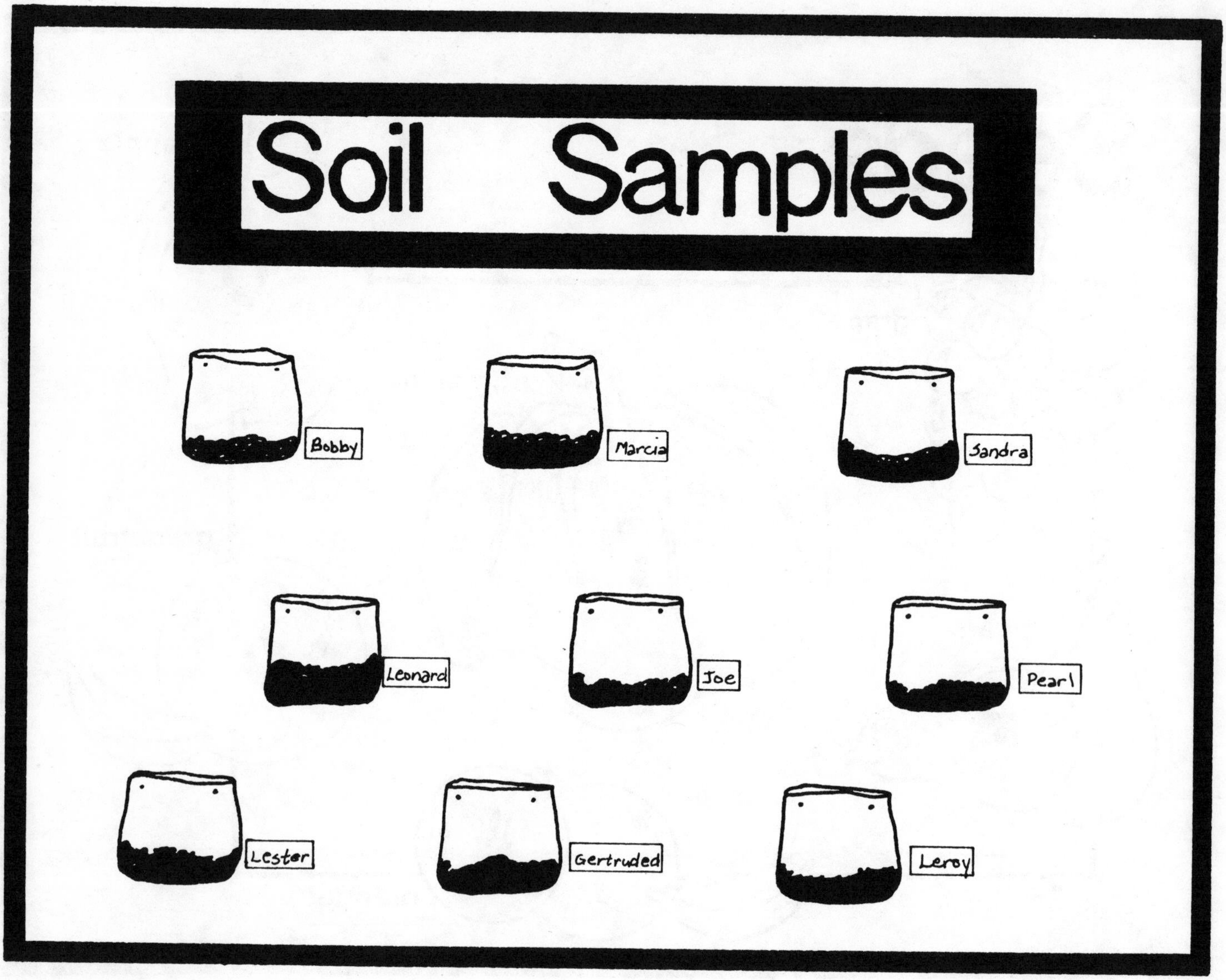

Soil Samples

Bobby

Marcia

Sandra

Leonard

Joe

Pearl

Lester

Gertruded

Leroy

Soil samples

Give children plastic bags to fill with soil found near their homes. When they bring their bags back to school, post them on the bulletin board. Take special note of color variations.

Sweetgum   dogwood   White oak   tulip poplar

trees

In autumn, draw three or four bare trees on the bulletin board. The trees should be indigenous to the area. Take the children for a walk to observe tree trunks and leaves. Collect several leaves from each tree.

After returning to the classroom, have the children make crayon rubbings of the leaves. (Use the rib side of the leaves for sharper outlines.) Then have them cut out the rubbings and tack them to the proper trees.

Alternative Method # 1: Trace patterns of leaves on colored construction paper, cut them out and tack them on the bulletin board.

Alternative Method # 2: Paint the rib side of leaves with tempera, then place them on clean newspaper. Place manila paper over each leaf and press or roll it with a brayer to make a clean print. When dry, cut the prints out and post them on the appropriate tree.

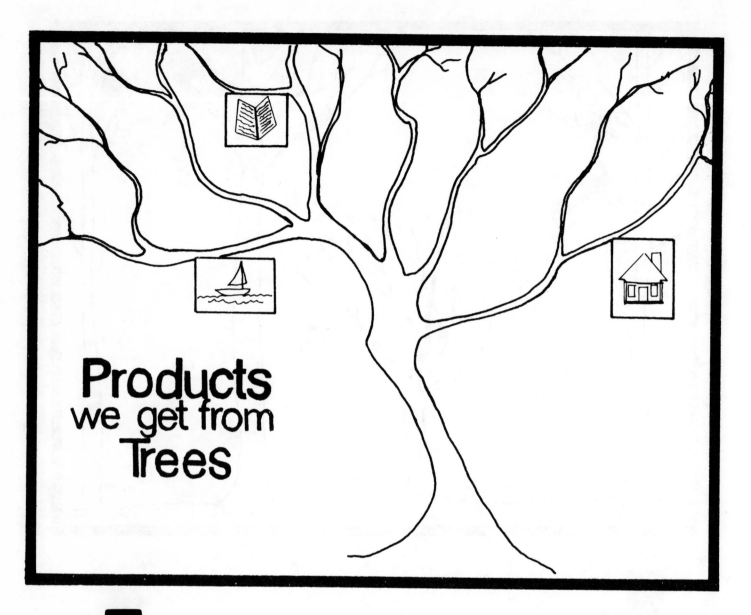

tree products

Make or tack a large drawing of a bare tree on the bulletin board. Give children magazines, scissors, colored construction paper and paste. Have them search for pictures of products derived from trees. The children cut out the pictures they find, mount them on colored construction paper and tack them on the branches of the trees.

Products might include: furniture, houses, boats, skis, pine straw, coconuts, and other fruit.

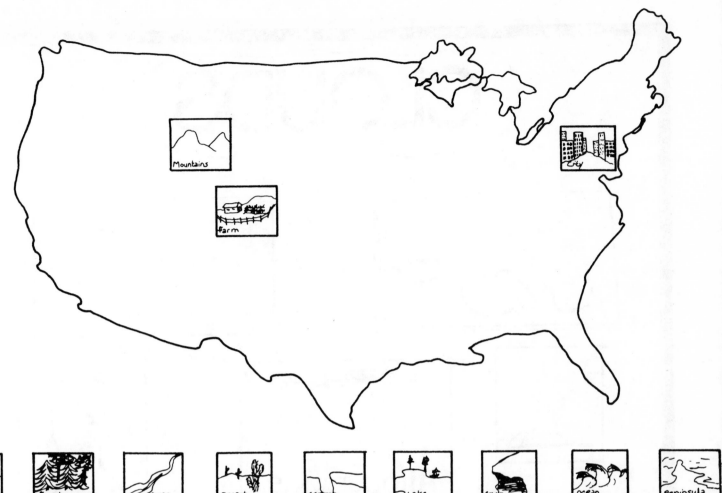

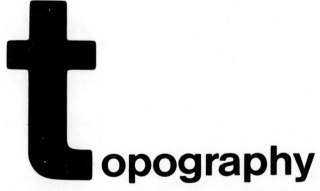

topography

Provide topographical pictures which the children are to place on the large map in appropriate spots. Have the children take turns working the bulletin board. You may wish to make additional picture cards, such as : prairie, volcano, bay, island, village, national park, etc.

Clouds

Lift panels display cloud formations on the outer flap. Children
try to identify clouds and check their answers by lifting the panel.
Cloud names are printed on the inner flap.

Weather

Weather *

When studying weather conditions, children may adjust the activities on this bulletin board several times during the day.

Place a real thermometer outside the classroom window and let children match the chart to it for a realistic reading.

* From *Early Childhood Activities: A Treasury of Ideas from Worldwide Sources* by Elaine Commins, M. Ed. Copyright © 1982 by Humanics Limited. Used with permission.

Wind

Have children look through old magazines to find "windy" pictures. Then have them cut out the pictures, mount them on colored construction paper and tack them on the bulletin board.

If desired, give children worksheets which contain two columns: one labeled "good," the other, "bad." In the "good" column, children list ways that the wind is helpful. In the "bad" column, they list wind's harmful effects.

The same type of bulletin board may be used for other weather conditions such as temperature, sunshine, and rainfall.

MAGNETS
follow directions

1.

foreign/domestic coins

Which coins are attracted to magnets?

2.

tacks   a clear plastic glass

Fill glass with water. Place tacks in glass. Do magnets attract under water?

3.

gem clips

String gem clips together. Compare how many gem clips each magnet attracts by adding to or subtracting from the chain.

4.

variety of objects

Which items such as a nail, chalk, small pencil, a key, staples, small scissors, cotton balls, a bandaide, etc. are attracted to the magnets?

magnets
(follow directions)

Tie strings around two or three different sized magnets and tack the strings to the bulletin board.

Post a series of experiments using the magnets. Have pairs of children take turns working them. As they finish each experiment, children remove the plastic bags from the board.

* Items such as a nail, chalk, small pencil, a key, staples, small scissors, cotton balls, a bandaid, etc.

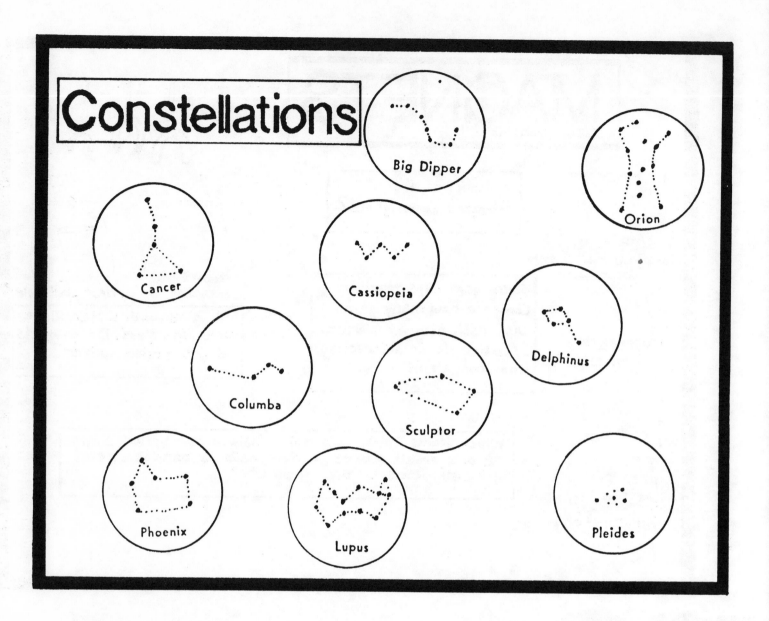

Constellations *

Display several constellation charts on the bulletin board. Give the children dark construction paper, chalk, glue, string, and gummed silver stars. Have them copy the constellations, making as many pictures as they desire. If you desire, staple a series of these papers together to form a booklet.

Which planet . . .

. . . is closest to the sun?	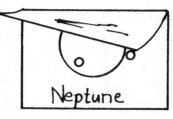 Neptune	. . . has rings
. . . is known as the red planet?	. . . is farthest from the sun?	. . . has an atmosphere?
. . . is the largest?	. . . has almost the same diameter as earth?	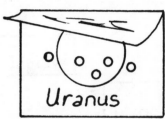 Uranus

Which planet...
(lift panels)

Gear the questions to the developmental level of the children. Some questions may have more than one answer.
For added interest, change questions daily.

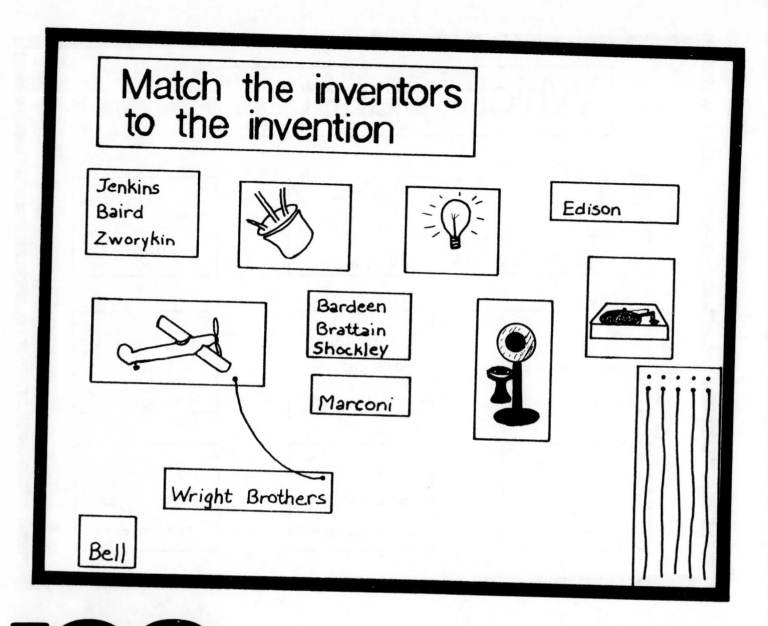

m

atch the inventors to the invention

Children connect the scientist to his or her invention with the various colored, heavy yarn supplied.

6

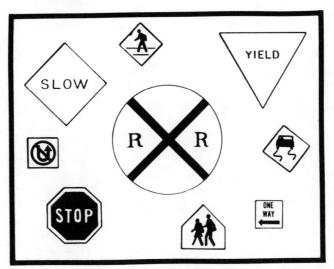

social studies

Social studies may include such diverse subjects as self-concepts, community workers, communication, transportation, history, economics, and government. The bulletin boards shown here are designed to enhance any ongoing units.

Sign up:
how do you feel today?

Self-concepts are important to young children. This kind of bulletin board can be effective when coordinated with class discussions. Change the sign up sheets each day.

 **he whole bloomin 1ˢᵗ grade**
(or kindergarten, etc.)

Prepare the bulletin board with a pale background (light blue or pink) and bright green stems and leaves. A rainbow caption is effective.

Give the children various colored construction paper and have them trace circles as flower centers and draw petals around the circles. Tack these flowers up on the green stem.

Then ask the children to bring a snapshot of themselves to school to be placed in the flower center. If you have a camera available, you may choose to take photographs of the children in the classroom.

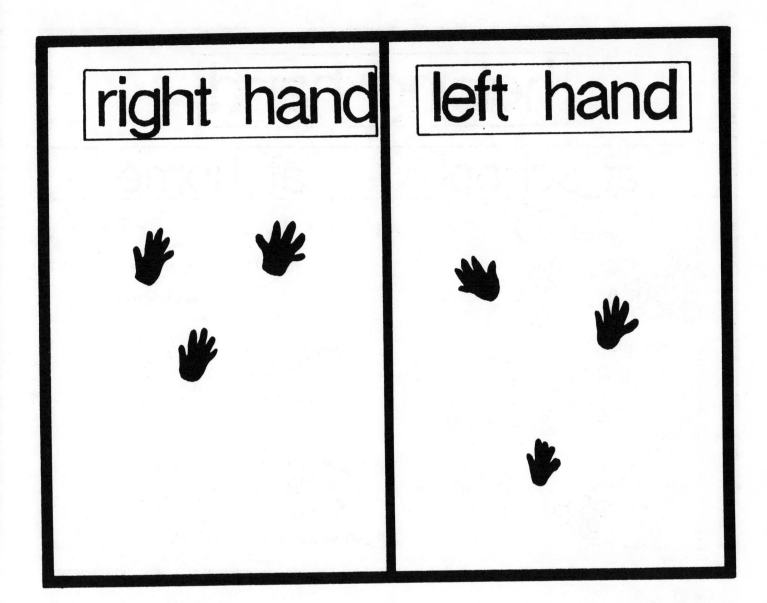

right hand / left hand

When teaching right / left handedness, have the children trace their right hands on one color construction paper and their left hands on another color. After cutting them out, the children post their hand cut-outs in the proper columns on the bulletin board.

helping hand

at school

Water plants — Laney

Wash tables — Donald

Sweep — Joe

at home

Donna

wash dishes

make bed — Fred

put away toys — Leslie

helping hands
at school / at home

If you so desire, post a small permanent bulletin in the room for weekly assignments. Parents might appreciate the carry-over duties in the home.

Furnish new hands each week or have children trace their own hands, cut them out, sign them and post them in the proper position on a weekly basis.

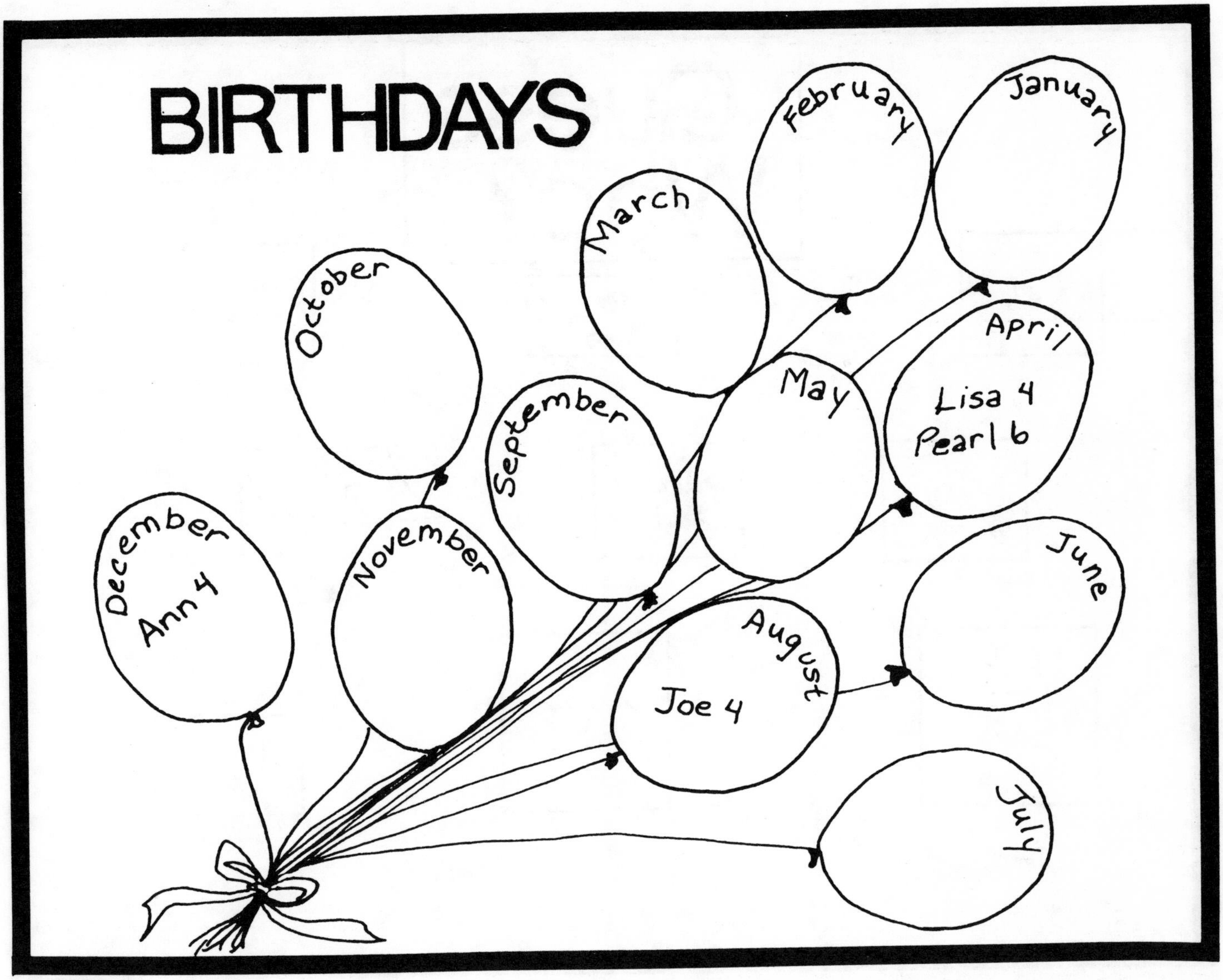
BIRTHDAYS
February
January
March
October
May
April
Lisa 4
Pearl 6
September
December
Ann 4
November
June
August
Joe 4
July

birthdays

With very young children, print names and ages on the balloons so the children can find their names on the bulletin board. Have older children write their names and birthdates on the appropriate balloon.

 **uess who?**

(lift-panels)

Ask the children to bring in one of their baby pictures. Glue or tape them to the outside flap of a lift-panel. Write the child's name on the inside.

Children try to guess each baby's identity.

designer clothes

Have children trace cardboard models of dolls, similar to the ones shown here, on heavy paper such as tagboard to make their own dolls. The dolls often develop into self-portraits.

Have children cut out doll clothes from colored construction paper, wallpaper or scrap material. Post clothes on the bulletin board.

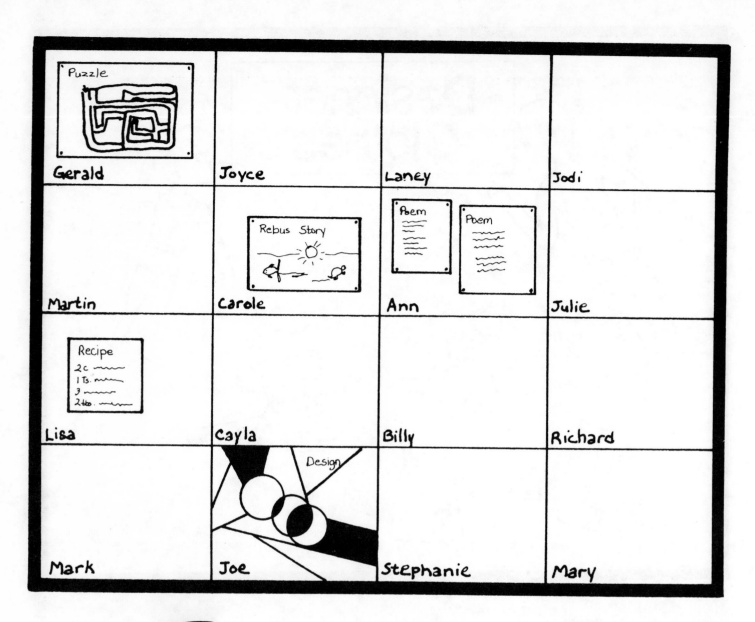

fill your own space

Divide the bulletin board into sections — one section for each child in the class. Allow each child to post personal material in his or her section.

Encourage creativity and individuality. Change sections as often as the child wishes.

  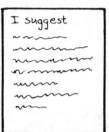 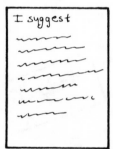

  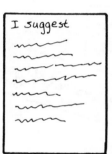

anonymous suggestions

Ask children to write suggestions, complaints or ideas about school, teachers, family, friends, etc. Instruct them *not* to sign their names. They may disguise their handwriting or choose a partner with whom they will exchange the task of writing their comments.

Allow two or three days to fill up the bulletin board.

On the fourth day, discuss the suggestions with the children and offer answers to the problems.

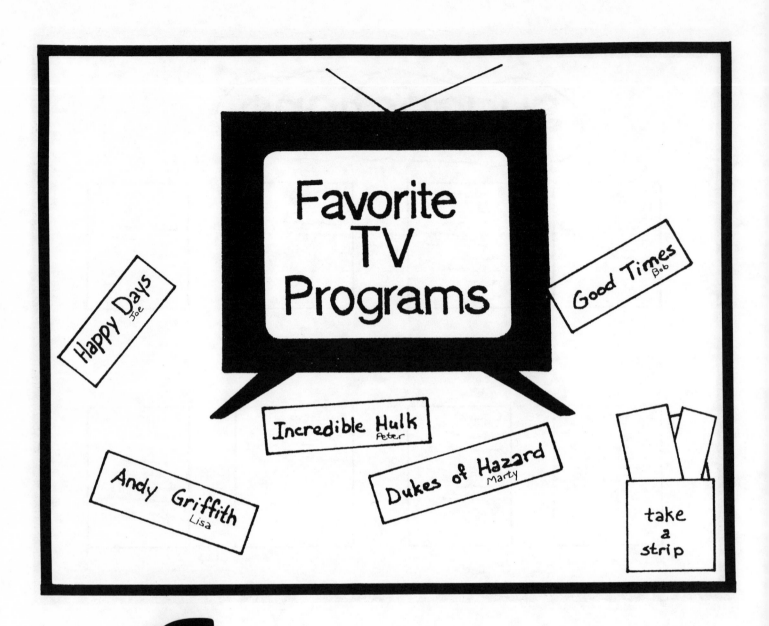

favorite (t.v.) programs

Each child takes a strip and writes his or her favorite TV program on it. After all strips have been posted, tally up the results.

Ways of coming to school			
🚌	👣	🚲	🚗
Carole	Martin	Laney	Philip
Julie	Gerald	Jodi	Lisa
Joyce			

Ways of coming to school *

Have children sign their names in the appropriate column.

* From *Early Childhood Activities: A Treasury of Ideas from Worldwide Sources* by Elaine Commins, M.Ed. Copyright 1982 by Humanics Limited. Used with permission.

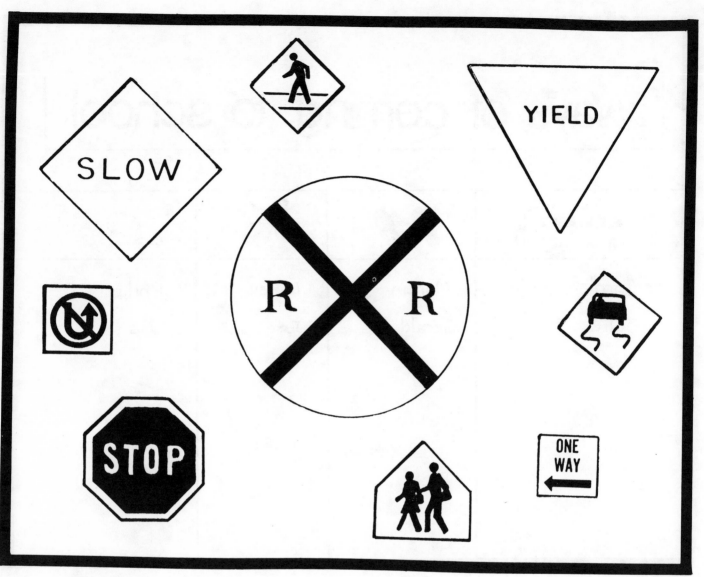

Safety signs

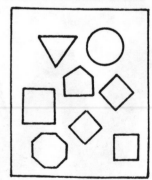

Fill the bulletin board with safety signs. Prepare an accompanying worksheet containing many shape-outlines similar to the shapes of the safety signs (see illustration). Give the children pencils, crayons and felt markers and have them fill in the empty shapes on their worksheets with letters and figures to match the safety signs.

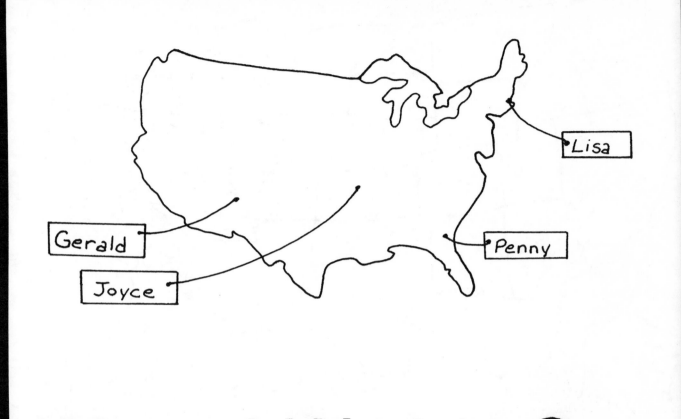

Where I Want to Go

Where I want to go *

Have the children post their names on the bulletin board, then connect their names to the place they wish to visit with colored yarn held in place with map tacks.

You may want to have upper grade students write the chamber of commerce in their chosen area and make a report for a social studies project.

map puzzle

Post a map of the United States showing only the outlines of states on the bulletin board. Prepare fifty posterboard puzzle pieces — either white or in various colors — each in the shape of a state. Label each piece with the name of the state. Tack a plastic bag to the board in which to store the puzzle pieces.

Have the children take turns individually or in pairs covering the outline map with matching states. Use map tacks or thumb tacks to hold the puzzle pieces in place.

indian tribes on the continental usa

This map indicates many of the Indian tribes and where they lived at the time of Columbus' arrival in the new world.

Ask the children to select one Indian tribe and find out all they can about it.

Who was
president
during
the War
of 1812?

Who was president
during the depression
of the 1930?

Thomas
Jefferson

President

Which
president
was a
rough rider?

Which president
was a college
president?

Who _____
_____ Civil War?
A. Lincoln

presidents

(lift panels)

Prepare a series of questions about American presidents. Print the questions on the outside of the lift panels and the answers on the inside. For optimum interest, change questions daily.

Other historical topics could also be treated in this manner, such as: explorers, battles, generals, kings, and queens.

meet the candidates

During an election campaign, prepare a bulletin board display of the various candidates. Ask each child to bring in an item — newspaper article, campaign button, bumper sticker, letter, etc. — concerning one of the candidates and post it in the appropriate space.

Further suggestions: Encourage upper grade students to write letters to candidates.

a mountain of wants *

Desires or needs for goods and services are basic economic concepts that can be taught to the youngest students.

Draw an outline of a mountain on the bulletin board. Give children old magazines and scissors. Have them cut out items they wish to own and tack them on the mountain. Draw lines around the items to keep them separate. Names on the items are optional.

* From *Early Childhood Activities: A Treasury of Ideas from Worldwide Sources* by Elaine Commins, M.Ed. Copyright © 1982 by Humanics Limited. Used with permission.

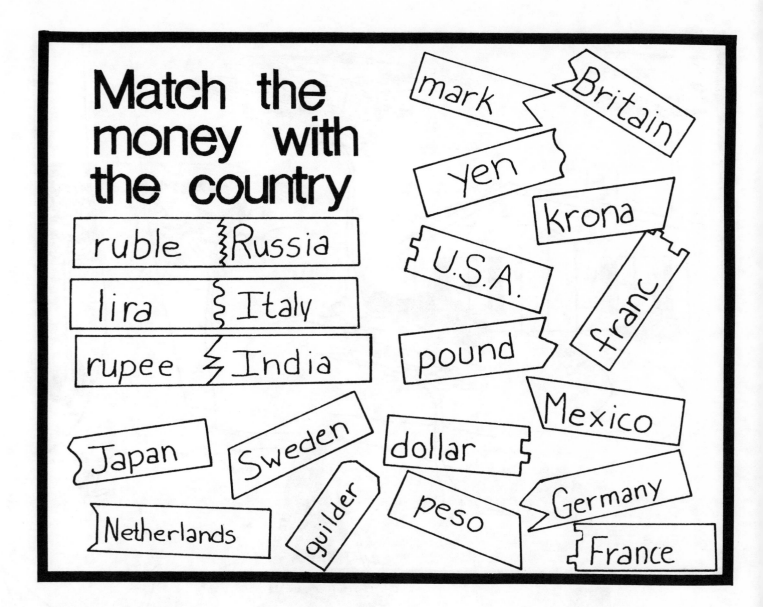

Match the money with the country

ruble } Russia

lira } Italy

rupee } India

mark

Britain

yen

krona

U.S.A.

franc

pound

Mexico

Japan

Sweden

dollar

guilder

peso

Germany

Netherlands

France

match the money with the country

Post the names of various currencies and their countries randomly over the bulletin board. Children take turns fitting the matching pairs together.

drama

Help children paint the background scenery for a play and post it on the bulletin board.

Children may also make their own costumes and masks. They can construct masks from paper plates. Let children take turns dramatizing the story.

7

Scary Mask

Contest

holidays

Holidays can encompass a wide variety of topics, such as famous birthdays, landmark discoveries, religious themes, patriotic occasions, seasonal celebrations or even days of festivity based on ancient superstitions and rituals.

What holiday comes in...

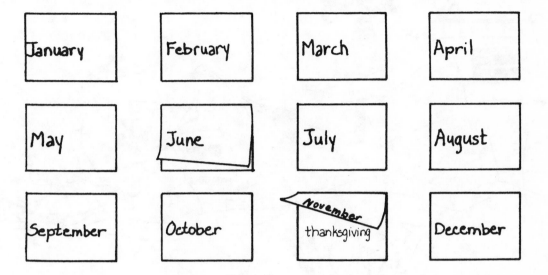

January	February	March	April
May	June	July	August
September	October	November thanksgiving	December

What holiday comes in...
(lift panels)

Dates of some holidays may vary each year. The following list is given for reference purposes:

JANUARY 1, New Years Day
     15, Martin Luther King's Birthday
     17, Ben Franklin's Birthday
FEBRUARY 2, Groundhog Day
     12, Abe Lincoln's Birthday
     14, Valentine's Day
     22, George Washington's Birthday
MARCH 22, Passover
     17, St. Patrick's Day
APRIL 1, April Fool's Day
     Easter
MAY 1, May Day
     2nd Sunday – Mother's Day
     Memorial Day

JUNE 14, Flag Day
     3rd Sunday – Father's Day
JULY 4, Independence Day
SEPTEMBER 1st Monday – Labor Day
     Rosh Hashanah
     Yom Kippur
OCTOBER 12, Columbus Day
     Sukkot
     31, Halloween
NOVEMBER 4th Thursday – Thanksgiving
DECEMBER   Chanukah
     25, Christmas

Christopher columbus and the sea monsters

The sailors on Christopher Columbus' ships believed that there were terrible sea monsters populating the ocean which would gobble up the ships. Have the children draw sea monsters and paint them, then cut them out and post them in the sea.

After all the sea monsters have been placed on the bulletin board, you may want to staple blue cellophane over the sea to create an eerie effect.

142

Scary Mask

Contest

Scary mask contest

Hold a scary mask contest at Halloween. Have each child construct a scary mask using a paper plate, paint, glitter, yarn, cotton balls, etc.

Take a vote after all entries have been posted. The prize is optional. Rather than a tangible prize, the winner might select the next game or activity.

THANKSGIVING

thanksgiving

Tack a posterboard turkey — without feathers — to the bulletin board. Give the children feather patterns to trace, paint and cut out. When the feathers dry, tack them around the turkey's body.

feather pattern

turkeys &

Post a bare turkey on the bulletin board. Give the children brown construction paper on which to trace their hands. They may paint the fingertips.

The children then cut out the hands and tack them to the bare turkey. (Hands should be tacked from the outer edge first).

trees

Draw the outline of a fir tree on the bulletin board. Give the children green construction paper on which to trace their hands.

For a winter tree, have the children paint the finger tips white. For a Christmas tree, have them glue glitter on the finger tips.

Children then cut out the hands and, beginning at the lowest branches, tack them to the tree.

letters to santa

As children mature, gifts received and gifts given should become more meaningful. Pose questions, such as: Why do they want the gift? Who will enjoy it, besides themselves? Will it last? Will it be remembered?

New Year's Resolutions

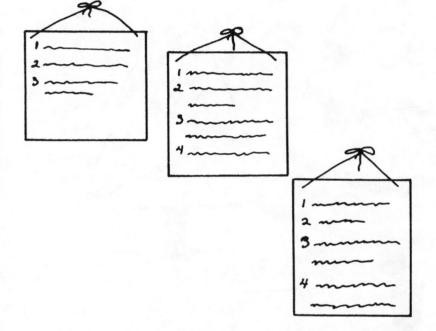
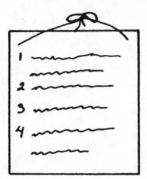

new year's resolutions

Have the children list their New Year's resolutions. Attach a ribbon tie to the top of each list. Then tack the bow of each tie to the bulletin board.

trim the tree

Tack an untrimmed tree on the bulletin board. Give children a variety of craft materials such as: glitter, metallic paper, colored cellophane paper, cotton balls, styrofoam shapes, paint, yarn, etc. They make and tack up their own tree decorations.

If there are two bulletin boards available in the room, post a large tree on each. Divide the class in half. Each half decorates one tree. This activity calls for preliminary planning by the groups.

Valentine bouquet

Post or draw a large flower bowl on the bulletin board. Give children heart stencils and a variety of craft materials such as red construction paper, crepe paper, glitter, paint, confetti, tissue paper, doilies, or colored cellophane paper. They decorate, cut out and post their hearts in the flower bowl.

Add leaves and stems, if desired.

love is...

Cover the bulletin board with red construction paper. Children trace and cut out their hands from white construction paper. Tack the hands to the board in the shape of a large heart.

Then ask the children to write a paragraph, a poem, or draw a picture of how they would describe love. Post these papers around the heart.

Encourage creativity!

name these great americans

George Washington's and Abraham Lincoln's birthdays are in February. They were great Americans. Children enjoy seeing their own silhouettes alongside the presidents'.

Using an overhead projector or a tensor lamp, trace each student's profile on white construction paper, cut it out and mount it on black construction paper. (If you prefer black silhouettes, staple a black piece of construction paper under the white paper drawing and cut out both papers at the same time.)

Have children try to guess the identity of each silhouette.

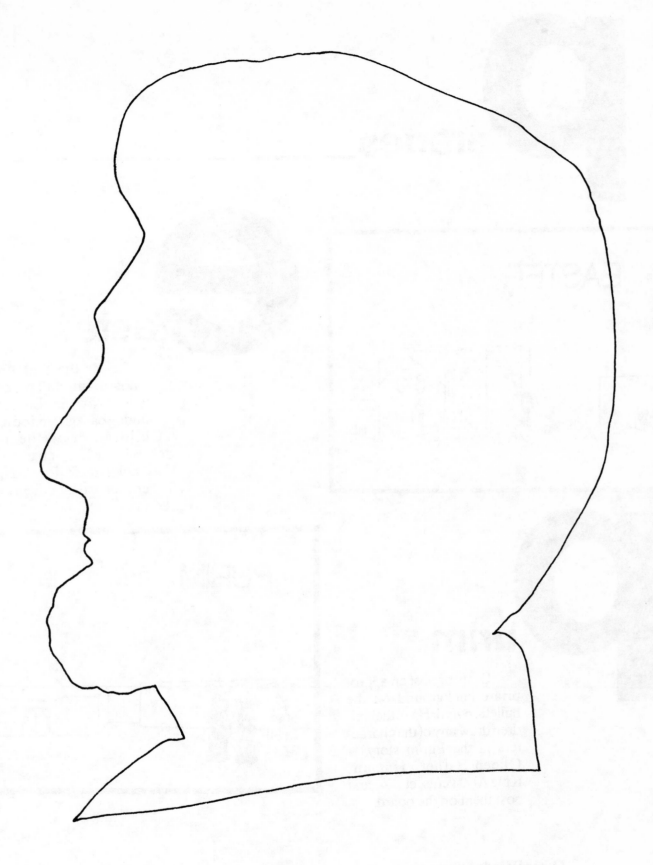

Parades

EASTER

easter

Cover the bulletin board with craft paper and draw an Easter Sunday background on it. Children draw themselves in the Easter parade. They color their drawings, cut them out and tack them to the board.

purim

Draw or post an appropriate background on the bulletin board. Have the children draw any of the characters in the Purim story — Queen Esther, Haman, King Ahasverus, etc. — and post them on the board.

PURIM

Other Parade Subjects:
Fourth of July, Labor Day, St. Patrick's Day, Freedom Marchers.

May Flowers

may day

may flowers

"Weave" a large bouquet with paper strips and wrapping paper and post it on the bulletin board.

Give children material to make a variety of leaves and flowers. Tissue paper, construction paper, crepe paper, straws, pipe cleaners, scissors and glue will spark creativity. Younger children need specific instructions.

m other's day bouquet

Give each child a flower shape made of construction paper. Put small squares (2" x 3") of various colored tissue paper on the art table. Have the children crumple and wad a tissue square, dip one side in glue and apply it to their construction paper flowers. The closer together the tissue paper wads, the more attractive the flower.

When finished, the children tack their flowers on the board.

Suggestion: Give children a pattern to trace and cut out for the border of this bulletin board.

how to make tissue paper flowers

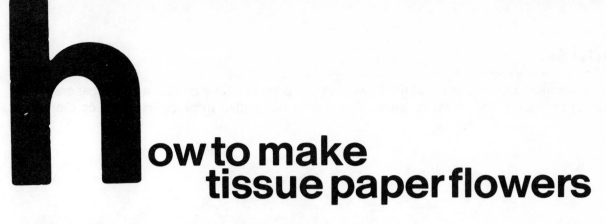

circles and pipe cleaners

1) Either trace or have the child trace and cut out colored tissue paper circles 4" or 5" in diameter.

2) Put four to seven tissue paper circles on one end of a pipe cleaner. "Knot" or curl the tip of the pipe cleaner to hold the petals (circles) in place.

3) Start with the petal nearest the pipe cleaner "knot" or curl and fold it up and squeeze it together, as shown.

4) Repeat this step with the second petal and each one after that.
Variation: You may spike or scallop the edges of the tissue paper circles.

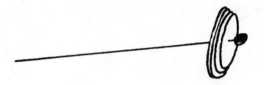

fringed tissue paper circles and straws

Either trace or have the child trace and cut out circles 4" or 5" in diameter. Have the children fringe the edges, cutting through three or four circles at a time. Then staple the circles to the end of a straw.

staple

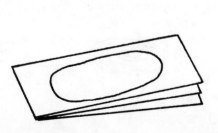

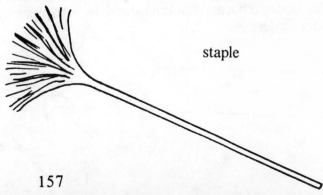

petals

Give children tissue paper petals. They glue one petal at a time around a pipe cleaner, beginning at the top and working down. Petals may be stapled in place to reinforce the glue.

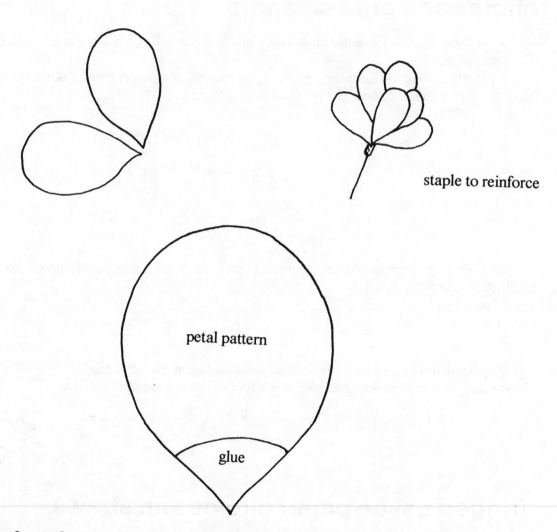

staple to reinforce

petal pattern

glue

folded strips of tissue paper and pipe cleaners

Children fold strips of tissue paper lengthwise, then wrap the strips around a finger. Pinch the bottom shut and staple it to hold. Insert a pipe cleaner as a stem. Use tape to hold it if necessary or desired.

staple

religious holidays

Divide the bulletin board into four or five sections, depending on the number of religions you'll be investigating. Give a list of religious holidays to the children. Tell them they may select one from the list, or one of their own choosing. Have them prepare a report on the holiday, telling its history and when and how it is celebrated. Post the reports in the appropriate section of the bulletin board.

Holidays and Festivals:

Christian — Christmas, St. Valentine's Day, Easter, and All Saint's Day

Jewish — Rosh Hashana, Yom Kippur, Succot, Chanukah, and Passover

Hindu — Hindu New Year, Krishna's birthday, Diwali (the Feast of Lights), and Holi

Buddhist — Wesak (the three main events in the life of Gautama), All Soul's Day or the Festival of Lanterns

Moslem — Ramadan, Maulid an-Nabi (the Prophet's birthday)

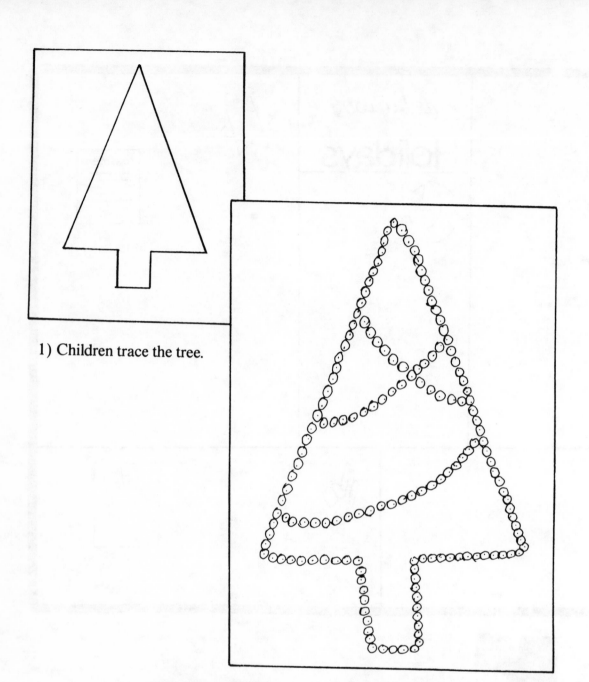

1) Children trace the tree.

2) Children stick gummed circles (reinforcers) on the outline. They may also use the circles to decorate the outline.

reinforce the holidays

Give the children patterns and stencils of holiday symbols. Have them trace the patterns on dark-colored construction paper, 8½" x 12".

Then have children stick gummed circles (reinforcers) on the outlines to make attractive pictures. They may tack their finished pictures on the holiday board.

For example, at Christmas, the following patterns could be used: trees, stars, reindeers, candelabras, and wreaths.

The Successful Teacher's Most Valuable Resource!

HUMANICS LIMITED

EDUCATION

THE EARLI PROGRAM
Excellent language development program! Volume I contains developmentally sequenced lessons in verbal receptive language; Volume II, expressive language. Use as a primary, supplemental or rehabilitative language program.

| Volume I | No. 067-7 | $14.95 |
| Volume II | No. 074-X | $14.95 |

LEARNING ENVIRONMENTS FOR CHILDREN
A practical manual for creating efficient, pleasant and stress-free learning environments for children centers. Make the best possible use of your center's space!

No. 065-0 $12.95

COMPETENCIES:
A Self-Study Guide to Teaching Competencies in Early Childhood Education
This comprehensive guide is ideal for evaluating or improving your competency in early childhood education or preparing for the CDA credential.

No. 024-3 $12.95

LOOKING AT CHILDREN:
Field Experiences in Child Study
A series of fourteen units made up of structured exercises dealing with such issues as language development, play and moral development in children. A fresh new approach to learning materials for early childhood educators.

No. 001-4 $12.95

YOUNG CHILDREN'S BEHAVIOR:
Implementing Your Goals
A variety of up-to-date approaches to discipline and guidance to help you deal more effectively with children. Also an excellent addition to CDA and competency-based training programs.

No. 015-4 $7.95

NUTS AND BOLTS
The ultimate guide to classroom organization and management of an early learning environment. Provides complete guidelines for setting up an early learning center; also excellent for improving an existing school system.

No. 063-4 $6.95

READING ROOTS:
Teach Your Child
Teach your child a basic reading vocabulary centered around the colors of his crayons before he enters school. Enjoyable coloring and matching activities make learning to read fun for both you and your child.

No. 070-7 $10.95

BACK TO BASICS IN READING MADE FUN
Refreshing and innovative approach to teaching basic reading skills which will delight and stimulate students. Over 100 creative games and projects to use in designing exciting reading materials.

No. 060-X $12.95

ACTIVITY BOOKS

EARLY CHILDHOOD ACTIVITIES:
A Treasury of Ideas from Worldwide Sources
A virtual encyclopedia of projects, games and activities for children aged 3 to 7, containing over 500 different child-tested activities drawn from a variety of teaching systems. The ultimate activity book!

No. 066-9 $16.95

VANILLA MANILA FOLDER GAMES
Make exciting and stimulating Vanilla Manila Folder Games quickly and easily with simple manila file folders and colored marking pens. Unique learning activities designed for children aged 3 to 8.

No. 059-6 $14.95

HANDBOOK OF LEARNING ACTIVITIES
Over 125 exciting, enjoyable activities and projects for young children in the areas of math, health and safety, play, movement, science, social studies, art, language development, puppetry and more!

No. 058-8 $14.95

MONTH BY MONTH ACTIVITY GUIDE FOR THE PRIMARY GRADES
Month by Month gives you a succinct guide to the effective recruitment and utilization of teachers' aides plus a full year's worth of fun-filled educational activities in such areas as reading, math, art, and science.

No. 061-8 $14.95

ART PROJECTS FOR YOUNG CHILDREN
Build a basic art program of stimulating projects on a limited budget and time schedule with Art Projects. Contains over 100 fun-filled projects in the areas of drawing, painting, puppets, clay, printing and more!

No. 051-0 $12.95

AEROSPACE PROJECTS FOR YOUNG CHILDREN
Introduce children to the fascinating field of aerospace with the exciting and informative projects and field trip suggestions. Contributors include over 30 aviation/aerospace agencies and personnel.

No. 052-9 $12.95

CHILD'S PLAY:
An Activities and Materials Handbook
An eclectic selection of fun-filled activities for preschool children designed to lend excitement to the learning process. Activities include puppets, mobiles, poetry, songs and more.

No. 003-0 $12.95

ENERGY:
A Curriculum for 3, 4 and 5 Year Olds
Help preschool children become aware of what energy is, the sources of energy, the uses of energy and wise energy use with the fun-filled activities, songs and games included in this innovative manual.

No. 069-3 $9.95

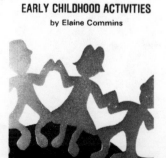

Humanics Publications

PARENT INVOLVEMENT

LOVE NOTES
A one year's supply of ready-to-use "Love Notes" to send home with the child to the parent. A novel and charming way to help parents enrich their parenting skills.

No. 068-5   **$19.95**

WORKING PARENTS:
How To Be Happy With Your Children
Dozens of easy and effective techniques and activities which will promote a constructive and enjoyable home and family life for the child and the working parent.

No. 006-5   **$7.95**

WORKING TOGETHER:
A Guide To Parent Involvement
Ideal guide for those wishing to launch a new parent involvement program or improve existing parent/school communication and interaction. Favorably reviewed by the National Association for Education of Young Children.

No. 003-0   **$12.95**

PARENTS AND TEACHERS
An intelligent, effective and field-tested program for improving the working relationship between parents and teachers. Now being used successfully in educational settings across the country.

No. 050-2   **$12.95**

ASSESSMENT

CHILDREN'S ADAPTIVE BEHAVIOR SCALE (CABS)
CABS is the first of its kind—a direct assessment tool which achieves the most complete measurement of adaptive behavior available today. Designed for children aged 5 to 11; quick and easy to administer.

No. 054-5   **$19.95**

THE LOLLIPOP TEST
A Diagnostic Screening Test of School Readiness
Based on the latest research in school readiness, this culture-free test effectively measures children's readiness strengths and weaknesses. Included is all you need to give, score and interpret the test.

No. 028-6   **$19.95**

H. N. PRESCHOOL ASSESSMENT HANDBOOK
Combines vital child development concepts into one integrated system of child observation and assessment. This is also the user's guide to the Humanics National Child Assessment Form—Age 3 to 6.

No. 020-0   **$16.95**

H. N. INFANT/TODDLER ASSESSMENT HANDBOOK
User's guide to the Humanics National Child Assessment Form—Age 0 to 3. Integrates critical concepts of child development into one effective system of observation and assessment.

No. 064-2   **$14.95**

SOCIAL SERVICES

HUMANICS LIMITED SYSTEM FOR RECORD KEEPING
Designed to meet <u>all</u> record keeping needs of family oriented social service agencies, this guide integrates the child, family, social worker and community into one coherent network. Also the user's guide to proper use of Humanics Limited Record Keeping forms.

No. 027-8   **$12.95**

REAL TALK:
Exercises in Friendship and Helping Skills
Real Talk teaches students basic skills in interpersonal relationships through such methods as role-playing and modeling. An ideal human relations course for elementary, junior high and high schools.

Teacher's Manual	No. 026-X	$ 7.95
Student's Manual	No. 025-1	$12.95

HUMANICS LIMITED

P.O. Box 7447
Atlanta, Georgia 30309
(404) 874-2176